D

b

PREFACE.

In describing the character and the action of the personages whose histories form the subjects of this series, the writer makes no attempt to darken the colors in which he depicts their deeds of violence and wrong, or to increase, by indignant denunciations, the obloquy which heroes and conquerors have so often brought upon themselves, in the estimation of mankind, by their ambition, their tyranny, or their desperate and reckless crimes. In fact, it seems desirable to diminish, rather than to increase, the spirit of censoriousness which often leads men so harshly to condemn the errors and sins of others, committed in circumstances of temptation to which they themselves were never exposed. Besides, to denounce or vituperate guilt, in a narrative of the transactions in which it was displayed, has little influence in awakening a healthy sensitiveness in the conscience of the reader. We observe, accordingly, that in the narratives of the sacred Scriptures, such denunciations are seldom found. The story of Absalom's undutifulness and rebellion, of David's adultery and murder, of Herod's tyranny, and all other narratives of crime, are related in a calm, simple, impartial, and forbearing spirit, which leads us to condemn the sins, but not to feel a pharisaical resentment and wrath against the sinner.

This example, so obviously proper and right, the writer of this series has made it his endeavor in all respects to follow.

CONTENTS.

Chapter

DARIUS THE GREAT

CHAPTER I.

CAMBYSES.

B.C. 530-524

Cyrus the Great.--His extended conquests.--Cambyses and Smerdis.--Hystaspes and Darius.--Dream of Cyrus.--His anxiety and fears.--Accession of Cambyses.--War with Egypt.--Origin of the war with Egypt.--Ophthalmia.--The Egyptian physician.--His plan of revenge.--Demand of Cyrus.--Stratagem of the King of Egypt.--Resentment of Cassandane.--Threats of Cambyses.--Future conquests.--Temperament and character of Cambyses.--Impetuosity of Cambyses.--Preparations for the Egyptian war.--Desertion of Phanes.--His narrow escape.--Information given by Phanes.--Treaty with the Arabian king.--Plan for providing water.--Account of Herodotus.--A great battle.--Defeat of the Egyptians.--Inhuman conduct of Cambyses.--His treatment of Psammenitus.--The train of captive maidens.--The young men.--Scenes of distress and suffering.--Composure of Psammenitus.--Feelings of the father.--His explanation of them.--Cambyses relents.--His treatment of the body of Amasis.--Cambyses's desecrations.--The sacred bull Apis.--Cambyses stabs the sacred bull.--His mad expeditions.--The sand storm.--Cambyses a wine-bibber.--Brutal act of Cambyses.--He is deemed insane.

About five or six hundred years before Christ, almost the whole of the interior of Asia was united in one vast empire. The founder of this empire was Cyrus the Great. He was originally a Persian; and the whole empire is often called the Persian monarchy, taking its name from its founder's native land.

Cyrus was not contented with having annexed to his dominion all the civilized states of Asia. In the latter part of his life, he conceived the idea that there might possibly be some additional glory and power to be acquired in subduing certain half-savage regions in the north, beyond the Araxes. He accordingly raised an army, and set off on an expedition for this purpose, against a country which was governed by a barbarian queen named Tomyris. He met with a variety of adventures on this expedition, all of which are fully detailed in our history of Cyrus. There is, however, only one occurrence that it is necessary to allude to particularly here. That one relates to a remarkable dream which he had one night, just after he had crossed the river.

To explain properly the nature of this dream, it is necessary first to state that Cyrus had two sons. Their names were Cambyses and Smerdis. He had left them in Persia when he set out on his expedition across the Araxes. There was also a young man, then about twenty years of age, in one of his capitals, named Darius. He was the son of one of the nobles of Cyrus's court. His father's name was Hystaspes. Hystaspes, besides being a noble of the court, was also, as almost all nobles were in those days, an officer of the army. He accompanied Cyrus in his march into the territories of the barbarian queen, and was with him there, in camp, at the time when this narrative commences.

Cyrus, it seems, felt some misgivings in respect to the result of his enterprise; and, in order to insure the tranquillity of his empire during his absence, and the secure transmission of his power to his rightful successor in case he should never return, he established his son Cambyses as regent of his realms before he crossed the Araxes, and delivered the government of the empire, with great formality, into his hands. This took place upon the frontier, just before the army passed the river. The mind of a father, under such circumstances, would naturally be occupied, in some degree, with thoughts relating to the arrangements which his son would make, and to the difficulties he would be likely to encounter in managing the momentous concerns which had been committed to his charge. The mind of Cyrus was undoubtedly so occupied, and this, probably, was the origin of the remarkable dream.

His dream was, that Darius appeared to him in a vision, with vast wings growing from his shoulders. Darius stood, in the vision, on the confines of Europe and Asia, and his wings, expanded either way, overshadowed the whole known world. When Cyrus awoke and reflected on this ominous dream, it seemed to him to portend some great danger to the future security of his empire. It appeared to denote that Darius was one day to bear sway over all the world. Perhaps he might be even then forming ambitious and treasonable designs. Cyrus immediately sent for Hystaspes, the father of Darius; when he came to his tent, he commanded him to go back to Persia, and keep a strict watch over the conduct of his son until he himself should return. Hystaspes received this commission, and departed to execute it; and Cyrus, somewhat relieved, perhaps, of his anxiety by this measure of precaution, went on with his army toward his place of destination.

Cyrus never returned. He was killed in battle; and it would seem that, though the import of his dream was ultimately fulfilled, Darius was not, at that time, meditating any schemes of obtaining possession of the throne, for he made no attempt to interfere with the regular transmission of the imperial power from Cyrus to Cambyses his son. At any rate, it was so transmitted. The tidings of Cyrus's death came to the capital, and Cambyses, his son, reigned in his stead.

The great event of the reign of Cambyses was a war with Egypt, which originated in the following very singular manner:

It has been found, in all ages of the world, that there is some peculiar quality of the soil, or climate, or atmosphere of Egypt which tends to produce an inflammation of the eyes. The inhabitants themselves have at all times been very subject to this disease, and foreign armies marching into the country are always very seriously affected by it. Thousands of soldiers in such armies are sometimes disabled from this cause, and many are made incurably blind. Now a country which produces a disease in its worst form and degree, will produce also, generally, the best physicians for that disease. At any rate, this was supposed to be the case in ancient times; and accordingly, when any powerful potentate in those days was afflicted himself with ophthalmia, or had such a case in his family, Egypt was the country to send to for a physician.

Now it happened that Cyrus himself, at one time in the course of his life, was attacked with this disease, and he dispatched an embassador to Amasis, who was then king of Egypt, asking him to send him a physician. Amasis, who, like all the other absolute sovereigns of those days, regarded his subjects as slaves that were in all respects entirely at his disposal, selected a physician of distinction from among the attendants about his court, and ordered him to repair to Persia. The physician was extremely reluctant to go. He had a wife and family, from whom he was very unwilling to be separated; but the orders were imperative, and he must obey. He set out on the journey, therefore, but he secretly resolved to devise some mode of revenging himself on the king for the cruelty of sending him.

He was well received by Cyrus, and, either by his skill as a physician, or from other causes, he acquired great influence at the Persian court. At last he contrived a mode of revenging himself on the Egyptian king for having exiled him from his native land. The king had a daughter, who was a lady of great beauty. Her father was very strongly attached to her. The physician recommended to Cyrus to send to Amasis and demand this daughter in marriage. As, however, Cyrus was already married, the Egyptian princess would, if she came, be his concubine rather than his wife, or, if considered a wife, it could only be a secondary and subordinate place that she could occupy. The physician knew that, under these circumstances, the King of Egypt would be extremely unwilling to send her to Cyrus, while he would yet scarcely dare to refuse; and the hope of plunging him into extreme embarrassment and distress, by means of such a demand from so powerful a sovereign, was the motive which led the physician to recommend the measure.

Cyrus was pleased with the proposal, and sent, accordingly, to make the demand. The king, as the physician had anticipated, could not endure to part with his daughter in such a way, nor did he, on the other hand, dare to incur the displeasure of so powerful a monarch by a direct and open refusal. He finally resolved upon escaping from the difficulty by a stratagem.

There was a young and beautiful captive princess in his court named Nitetis. Her father, whose name was Apries, had been formerly the King of Egypt, but he had been dethroned and killed by Amasis. Since the downfall of her family, Nitetis had been a captive; but, as she was very beautiful and very accomplished, Amasis conceived the design of sending her to Cyrus, under the pretense that she was the daughter whom Cyrus had demanded. He accordingly brought her forth, provided her with the most costly and splendid dresses, loaded her with presents, ordered a large retinue to attend her, and sent her forth to Persia.

Cyrus was at first very much pleased with his new bride. Nitetis became, in fact, his principal favorite; though, of course, his other wife, whose name was Cassandane, and her children, Cambyses and Smerdis, were jealous of her, and hated her. One day, a Persian lady was visiting at the court, and as she was standing near Cassandane, and saw her two sons, who were then tall and handsome young men, she expressed her admiration of them, and said to

Cassandane, "How proud and happy you must be!" "No," said Cassandane; "on the contrary, I am very miserable; for, though I am the mother of these children, the king neglects and despises me. All his kindness is bestowed on this Egyptian woman." Cambyses, who heard this conversation, sympathized deeply with Cassandane in her resentment. "Mother," said he, "be patient, and I will avenge you. As soon as I am king, I will go to Egypt and turn the whole country upside down."

In fact, the tendency which there was in the mind of Cambyses to look upon Egypt as the first field of war and conquest for him, so soon as he should succeed to the throne, was encouraged by the influence of his father; for Cyrus, although he was much captivated by the charms of the lady whom the King of Egypt had sent him, was greatly incensed against the king for having practiced upon him such a deception. Besides, all the important countries in Asia were already included within the Persian dominions. It was plain that if any future progress were to be made in extending the empire, the regions of Europe and Africa must be the theatre of it. Egypt seemed the most accessible and vulnerable point beyond the confines of Asia; and thus, though Cyrus himself, being advanced somewhat in years, and interested, moreover, in other projects, was not prepared to undertake an enterprise into Africa himself, he was very willing that such plans should be cherished by his son.

Cambyses was an ardent, impetuous, and self-willed boy, such as the sons of rich and powerful men are very apt to become. They imbibe, by a sort of sympathy, the ambitious and aspiring spirit of their fathers; and as all their childish caprices and passions are generally indulged, they never learn to submit to control. They become vain, self-conceited, reckless, and cruel. The conqueror who founds an empire, although even his character generally deteriorates very seriously toward the close of his career, still usually knows something of moderation and generosity. His son, however, who inherits his father's power, seldom inherits the virtues by which the power was acquired. These truths, which we see continually exemplified all around us, on a small scale, in the families of the wealthy and the powerful, were illustrated most conspicuously, in the view of all mankind, in the case of Cyrus and Cambyses. The father was prudent, cautious, wise, and often generous and forbearing. The son grew up headstrong, impetuous, uncontrolled, and uncontrollable. He had the most lofty ideas of his own greatness and power, and he felt a supreme contempt for the rights, and indifference to the happiness of all the world besides. His history gives us an illustration of the worst which the principle of hereditary sovereignty can do, as the best is exemplified in the case of Alfred of England.

Cambyses, immediately after his father's death, began to make arrangements for the Egyptian invasion. The first thing to be determined was the mode of transporting his armies thither. Egypt is a long and narrow valley, with the rocks and deserts of Arabia on one side, and those of Sahara on the other. There is no convenient mode of access to it except by sea, and Cambyses had no naval force sufficient for a maritime expedition.

While he was revolving the subject in his mind, there arrived in his capital of Susa, where he was then residing, a deserter from the army of Amasis in Egypt. The name of this deserter was Phanes. He was a Greek, having been the commander of a body of Greek troops who were employed by Amasis as auxiliaries in his army. He had had a quarrel with Amasis, and had fled to Persia, intending to join Cambyses in the expedition which he was contemplating, in order to revenge himself on the Egyptian king. Phanes said, in telling his story, that he had had a very narrow escape from Egypt; for, as soon as Amasis had heard that he had fled, he dispatched one of his swiftest vessels, a galley of three banks of oars, in hot pursuit of the fugitive. The galley overtook the vessel in which Phanes had taken passage just as it was landing in Asia Minor. The Egyptian officers seized it and made Phanes prisoner. They immediately began to make their preparations for the return voyage, putting Phanes, in the mean time, under the charge of guards, who were instructed to keep him very safely. Phanes, however, cultivated a good understanding with his guards, and presently invited them to drink wine with him. In the end, he got them intoxicated, and while they were in that state he made his escape from them, and then, traveling with great secrecy and caution until he was beyond their reach, he succeeded in making his way to Cambyses in Susa.

Phanes gave Cambyses a great deal of information in respect to the geography of Egypt, the proper points of attack, the character and resources of the king, and communicated, likewise, a great many other particulars which it was very important that Cambyses should know. He recommended that Cambyses should proceed to Egypt by land, through Arabia; and that, in order to secure a safe passage, he should send first to the King of the Arabs, by a formal embassy, asking permission to cross his territories with an army, and engaging the Arabians to aid him, if possible, in the transit. Cambyses did this. The Arabs were very willing to join in any projected hostilities against the Egyptians; they offered Cambyses a free passage, and agreed to aid his army on their march. To the faithful fulfillment of these stipulations the Arab chief bound himself by a treaty, executed with the most solemn forms and ceremonies.

The great difficulty to be encountered in traversing the deserts which Cambyses would have to cross on his way to Egypt was the want of water. To provide for this necessity, the king of the Arabs sent a vast number of camels into the desert, laden with great sacks or bags full of water. These camels were sent forward just before the army of Cambyses came on, and they deposited their supplies along the route at the points where they would be most needed. Herodotus, the Greek traveler, who made a journey into Egypt not a great many years after these transactions, and who wrote subsequently a full description of what he saw and heard there, gives an account of another method by which the Arab king was said to have conveyed water into the desert, and that was by a canal or pipe, made of the skins of oxen, which he laid along the ground, from a certain river of his dominions, to a distance of twelve days' journey over the sands! This story Herodotus says he did not believe, though elsewhere in the course of his history he gravely relates, as true history, a thousand tales infinitely more improbable than the idea of a leathern pipe or hose like this to serve for a conduit of water.

By some means or other, at all events, the Arab chief provided supplies of water in the desert for Cambyses's army, and the troops made the passage safely. They arrived, at length, on the frontiers of Egypt.[A] Here they found that Amasis, the king, was dead, and Psammenitus, his son, had succeeded him. Psammenitus came forward to meet the invaders. A great battle was fought. The Egyptians were routed. Psammenitus fled up the Nile to the city of Memphis, taking with him such broken remnants of his army as he could get together after the battle, and feeling extremely incensed and exasperated against the invader. In fact, Cambyses had now no excuse or pretext whatever for waging such a war against Egypt. The monarch who had deceived his father was dead, and there had never been any cause of complaint against his son or against the Egyptian people. Psammenitus, therefore, regarded the invasion of Egypt by Cambyses as a wanton and wholly unjustifiable aggression, and he determined, in his own mind, that such invaders deserved no mercy, and that he would show them none. Soon after this, a galley on the river, belonging to Cambyses, containing a crew of two hundred men, fell into his hands. The Egyptians, in their rage, tore these Persians all to pieces. This exasperated Cambyses in his turn, and the war went on, attended by the most atrocious cruelties on both sides.

[Footnote A: For the places mentioned in this chapter, and the track of Cambyses on his expedition, see the map at the commencement of this volume.]

In fact, Cambyses, in this Egyptian campaign, pursued such a career of inhuman and reckless folly, that people at last considered him insane. He began with some small semblance of moderation, but he proceeded, in the end, to the perpetration of the most terrible excesses of violence and wrong.

As to his moderation, his treatment of Psammenitus personally is almost the only instance that we can record. In the course of the war, Psammenitus and all his family fell into Cambyses's hands as captives. A few days afterward, Cambyses conducted the unhappy king without the gates of the city to exhibit a spectacle to him. The spectacle was that of his beloved daughter, clothed in the garments of a slave, and attended by a company of other maidens, the daughters of the nobles and other persons of distinction belonging to his court, all going down to the river, with heavy jugs, to draw water. The fathers of all these hapless maidens had been brought out with Psammenitus to witness the degradation and misery of their children. The maidens cried and sobbed aloud as they went along, overwhelmed with shame and terror. Their fathers manifested the utmost agitation and distress. Cambyses stood smiling by, highly enjoying the spectacle. Psammenitus alone appeared unmoved. He gazed on the scene silent, motionless, and with a countenance which indicated no active suffering; he seemed to be in a state of stupefaction and despair. Cambyses was disappointed, and his pleasure was marred at finding that his victim did not feel more acutely the sting of the torment with which he was endeavoring to goad him.

When this train had gone by, another came. It was a company of young men, with halters about their necks, going to execution. Cambyses had ordered that for every one of the crew of his galley that the Egyptians had killed, ten

Egyptians should be executed. This proportion would require two thousand victims, as there had been two hundred in the crew. These victims were to be selected from among the sons of the leading families; and their parents, after having seen their delicate and gentle daughters go to their servile toil, were now next to behold their sons march in a long and terrible array to execution. The son of Psammenitus was at the head of the column. The Egyptian parents who stood around Psammenitus wept and lamented aloud, as one after another saw his own child in the train. Psammenitus himself, however, remained as silent and motionless, and with a countenance as vacant as before. Cambyses was again disappointed. The pleasure which the exhibition afforded him was incomplete without visible manifestations of suffering in the victim for whose torture it was principally designed.

After this train of captives had passed, there came a mixed collection of wretched and miserable men, such as the siege and sacking of a city always produces in countless numbers. Among these was a venerable man whom Psammenitus recognized as one of his friends. He had been a man of wealth and high station; he had often been at the court of the king, and had been entertained at his table. He was now, however, reduced to the last extremity of distress, and was begging of the people something to keep him from starving. The sight of this man in such a condition seemed to awaken the king from his blank and death-like despair. He called his old friend by name in a tone of astonishment and pity, and burst into tears.

Cambyses, observing this, sent a messenger to Psammenitus to inquire what it meant. "He wishes to know," said the messenger, "how it happens that you could see your own daughter set at work as a slave, and your son led away to execution unmoved, and yet feel so much commiseration for the misfortunes of a stranger." We might suppose that any one possessing the ordinary susceptibilities of the human soul would have understood without an explanation the meaning of this, though it is not surprising that such a heartless monster as Cambyses did not comprehend it. Psammenitus sent him word that he could not help weeping for his friend, but that his distress and anguish on account of his children were too great for tears.

The Persians who were around Cambyses began now to feel a strong sentiment of compassion for the unhappy king, and to intercede with Cambyses in his favor. They begged him, too, to spare Psammenitus's son. It will interest those of our readers who have perused our history of Cyrus to know that Croesus, the captive king of Lydia, whom they will recollect to have been committed to Cambyses's charge by his father, just before the close of his life, when he was setting forth on his last fatal expedition, and who accompanied Cambyses on this invasion of Egypt, was present on this occasion, and was one of the most earnest interceders in Psammenitus's favor. Cambyses allowed himself to be persuaded. They sent off a messenger to order the execution of the king's son to be stayed; but he arrived too late. The unhappy prince had already fallen. Cambyses was so far appeased by the influence of these facts, that he abstained from doing Psammenitus or his family any further injury.

He, however, advanced up the Nile, ravaging and plundering the country as he went on, and at length, in the course of his conquests, he gained possession of the tomb in which the embalmed body of Amasis was deposited. He ordered this body to be taken out of its sarcophagus, and treated with every mark of ignominy. His soldiers, by his orders, beat it with rods, as if it could still feel, and goaded it, and cut it with swords. They pulled the hair out of the head by the roots, and loaded the lifeless form with every conceivable mark of insult and ignominy. Finally, Cambyses ordered the mutilated remains that were left to be burned, which was a procedure as abhorrent to the ideas and feelings of the Egyptians as could possibly be devised.

Cambyses took every opportunity to insult the religious, or as, perhaps, we ought to call them, the superstitious feelings of the Egyptians. He broke into their temples, desecrated their altars, and subjected every thing which they held most sacred to insult and ignominy. Among their objects of religious veneration was the sacred bull called Apis. This animal was selected from time to time, from the country at large, by the priests, by means of certain marks which they pretended to discover upon its body, and which indicated a divine and sacred character. The sacred bull thus found was kept in a magnificent temple, and attended and fed in a most sumptuous manner. In serving him, the attendants used vessels of gold.

Cambyses arrived at the city where Apis was kept at a time when the priests were celebrating some sacred occasion with festivities and rejoicings. He was himself then returning from an unsuccessful expedition which he had made, and, as he entered the town, stung with vexation and anger at his defeat, the gladness and joy which the Egyptians manifested in their ceremonies served only to irritate him, and to make him more angry than ever. He killed the priests who were officiating. He then demanded to be taken into the edifice to see the sacred animal, and there, after insulting the feelings of the worshipers in every possible way by ridicule and scornful words, he stabbed the innocent bull with his dagger. The animal died of the wound, and the whole country was filled with horror and indignation. The people believed that this deed would most assuredly bring down upon the impious perpetrator of it the judgments of heaven.

Cambyses organized, while he was in Egypt, several mad expeditions into the surrounding countries. In a fit of passion, produced by an unsatisfactory answer to an embassage, he set off suddenly, and without any proper preparation, to march into Ethiopia. The provisions of his army were exhausted before he had performed a fifth part of the march. Still, in his infatuation, he determined to go on. The soldiers subsisted for a time on such vegetables as they could find by the way; when these failed, they slaughtered and ate their beasts of burden; and finally, in the extremity of their famine, they began to kill and devour one another; then, at length, Cambyses concluded to return. He sent off, too, at one time, a large army across the desert toward the Temple of Jupiter Ammon, without any of the necessary precautions for such a march. This army never reached their destination, and they never returned. The people of the Oasis said that they were overtaken by a sand storm in the desert, and were all overwhelmed.

There was a certain officer in attendance on Cambyses named Prexaspes. He was a sort of confidential friend and companion of the king; and his son, who was a fair, and graceful, and accomplished youth, was the king's cup-bearer, which was an office of great consideration and honor. One day Cambyses asked Prexaspes what the Persians generally thought of him. Prexaspes replied that they thought and spoke well of him in all respects but one. The king wished to know what the exception was. Prexaspes rejoined, that it was the general opinion that he was too much addicted to wine. Cambyses was offended at this reply; and, under the influence of the feeling, so wholly unreasonable and absurd, which so often leads men to be angry with the innocent medium through which there comes to them any communication which they do not like, he determined to punish Prexaspes for his freedom.

He ordered his son, therefore, the cup-bearer, to take his place against the wall on the other side of the room. "Now," said he, "I will put what the Persians say to the test." As he said this, he took up a bow and arrow which were at his side, and began to fit the arrow to the string. "If," said he, "I do not shoot him exactly through the heart, it shall prove that the Persians are right. If I do, then they are wrong, as it will show that I do not drink so much as to make my hand unsteady." So saying, he drew the bow, the arrow flew through the air and pierced the poor boy's breast. He fell, and Cambyses coolly ordered the attendants to open the body, and let Prexaspes see whether the arrow had not gone through the heart.

These, and a constant succession of similar acts of atrocious and reckless cruelty and folly, led the world to say that Cambyses was insane.

CHAPTER II.

THE END OF CAMBYSES.

B.C. 523-522

Cambyses's profligate conduct.--He marries his own sisters.--Consultation of the Persian judges.--Their opinion.--Smerdis.--Jealousy of Cambyses.--The two magi.--Cambyses suspicious.--He plans an invasion of Ethiopia.--Island of Elephantine.--The Icthyophagi.--Classes of savage nations.--Embassadors sent to Ethiopia.--The presents.--The Ethiopian king detects the imposture.--The Ethiopian king's opinion of Cambyses's presents.--The Ethiopian bow.--Return of the Icthyophagi.--Jealousy of Cambyses.--He orders Smerdis to be murdered.--Cambyses grows more cruel.--Twelve noblemen buried alive.-- Cambyses's cruelty to his sister.--Her death.--The venerable Croesus.--His advice to Cambyses.--Cambyses's rage at Croesus.--He attempts to kill him.-- The declaration of the oracle.--Ecbatane, Susa, and Babylon.--Cambyses returns northward.--He enters Syria.--A herald proclaims Smerdis.--The herald seized.--Probable explanation.--Rage of Cambyses.--Cambyses mortally wounded.--His remorse and despair.--Cambyses calls his nobles about him.-- His dying declaration.--Death of Cambyses.--His dying declaration discredited.

Among the other acts of profligate wickedness which have blackened indelibly and forever Cambyses's name, he married two of his own sisters, and brought one of them with him to Egypt as his wife. The natural instincts of all men, except those whose early life has been given up to the most shameless and dissolute habits of vice, are sufficient to preserve them from such crimes as these. Cambyses himself felt, it seems, some misgivings when contemplating the first of these marriages; and he sent to a certain council of judges, whose province it was to interpret the laws, asking them their opinion of the rightfulness of such a marriage. Kings ask the opinion of their legal advisers in such cases, not because they really wish to know whether the act in question is right or wrong, but because, having themselves determined upon the performance of it, they wish their counselors to give it a sort of legal sanction, in order to justify the deed, and diminish the popular odium which it might otherwise incur.

The Persian judges whom Cambyses consulted on this occasion understood very well what was expected of them. After a grave deliberation, they returned answer to the king that, though they could find no law allowing a man to marry his sister, they found many which authorized a king of Persia to do whatever he thought best. Cambyses accordingly carried his plan into execution. He married first the older sister, whose name was Atossa. Atossa became subsequently a personage of great historical distinction. The daughter of Cyrus, the wife of Darius, and the mother of Xerxes, she was the link that bound together the three most magnificent potentates of the whole Eastern world. How far these sisters were willing participators in the guilt of their incestuous marriages we can not now know. The one who went with Cambyses into Egypt was of a humane, and gentle, and timid disposition, being in these respects wholly unlike her brother; and it may be that she merely yielded, in the transaction of her marriage, to her brother's arbitrary and imperious will.

Besides this sister, Cambyses had brought his brother Smerdis with him into Egypt. Smerdis was younger than Cambyses, but he was superior to him in strength and personal accomplishments. Cambyses was very jealous of this superiority. He did not dare to leave his brother in Persia, to manage the government in his stead during his absence, lest he should take advantage of the temporary power thus committed to his hands, and usurp the throne altogether. He decided, therefore, to bring Smerdis with him into Egypt, and to leave the government of the state in the hands of a regency composed of two magi. These magi were public officers of distinction, but, having no hereditary claims to the crown, Cambyses thought there would be little danger of their attempting to usurp it. It happened, however, that the name of one of these magi was Smerdis. This coincidence between the magian's name and that of the prince led, in the end, as will presently be seen, to very important consequences.

The uneasiness and jealousy which Cambyses felt in respect to his brother was not wholly allayed by the arrangement which he thus made for keeping him in his army, and so under his own personal observation and command. Smerdis evinced, on various occasions, so much strength and skill, that Cambyses feared his influence among the officers and soldiers, and was rendered continually watchful, suspicious, and afraid. A circumstance at last occurred which excited his jealousy more than ever, and he determined to send Smerdis home again to Persia. The circumstance was this:

After Cambyses had succeeded in obtaining full possession of Egypt, he formed, among his other wild and desperate schemes, the design of invading the territories of a nation of Ethiopians who lived in the interior of Africa, around and beyond the sources of the Nile. The Ethiopians were celebrated for their savage strength and bravery. Cambyses wished to obtain information respecting them and their country before setting out on his expedition against them, and he determined to send spies into their country to obtain it. But, as Ethiopia was a territory so remote, and as its institutions and customs, and the language, the dress, and the manners of its inhabitants were totally different from those of all the other nations of the earth, and were almost wholly unknown to the Persian army, it was impossible to send Persians in disguise, with any hope that they could enter and explore the country without being discovered. It was very doubtful, in fact, whether, if such spies were to be sent, they could succeed in reaching Ethiopia at all.

Now there was, far up the Nile, near the cataracts, at a place where the river widens and forms a sort of bay, a large and fertile island called Elephantine, which was inhabited by a half-savage tribe called the Icthyophagi. They lived mainly by fishing on the river, and, consequently, they had many boats, and were accustomed to make long excursions up and down the stream. Their name was, in fact, derived from their occupation. It was a Greek word, and might be translated "Fishermen."[B] The manners and customs of half-civilized or savage nations depend entirely, of course, upon the modes in which they procure their subsistence. Some depend on hunting wild beasts, some on rearing flocks and herds of tame animals, some on cultivating the ground, and some on fishing in rivers or in the sea. These four different modes of procuring food result in as many totally diverse modes of life: it is a curious fact, however, that while a nation of hunters differs very essentially from a nation of herdsmen or of fishermen, though they may live, perhaps, in the same neighborhood with them, still, all nations of hunters, however widely they may be separated in geographical position, very strongly resemble one another in character, in customs, in institutions, and in all the usages of life. It is so, moreover, with all the other types of national constitution mentioned above. The Greeks observed these characteristics of the various savage tribes with which they became acquainted, and whenever they met with a tribe that lived by fishing, they called them Icthyophagi.

[Footnote B: Literally, fish-eaters.]

Cambyses sent to the Icthyophagi of the island of Elephantine, requiring them to furnish him with a number of persons acquainted with the route to Ethiopia and with the Ethiopian language, that he might send them as an embassy. He also provided some presents to be sent as a token of friendship to the Ethiopian king. The presents were, however, only a pretext, to enable the embassadors, who were, in fact, spies, to go to the capital and court of the Ethiopian monarch in safety, and bring back to Cambyses all the information which they should be able to obtain.

The presents consisted of such toys and ornaments as they thought would most please the fancy of a savage king. There were some purple vestments of a very rich and splendid dye, and a golden chain for the neck, golden bracelets for the wrists, an alabaster box of very precious perfumes, and other similar trinkets and toys. There was also a large vessel filled with wine.

The Icthyophagi took these presents, and set out on their expedition. After a long and toilsome voyage and journey, they came to the country of the Ethiopians, and delivered their presents, together with the message which Cambyses had intrusted to them. The presents, they said, had been sent by Cambyses as a token of his desire to become the friend and ally of the Ethiopian king.

The king, instead of being deceived by this hypocrisy, detected the imposture at once. He knew very well, he said, what was the motive of Cambyses in sending such an embassage to him, and he should advise Cambyses to be content with his own dominions, instead of planning aggressions of violence, and schemes and stratagems of deceit against his neighbors, in order to get possession of theirs. He then began to look at the presents which the embassadors had brought, which, however, he appeared very soon to despise. The purple vest first attracted his attention. He asked whether that was the true, natural color of the stuff, or a false one. The messengers told him that the linen was dyed, and began to explain the process to him. The mind of the savage potentate, however, instead of being impressed, as the messengers supposed he would have been through their description, with a high idea of the excellence and superiority of Persian art, only despised the false show of what he considered an artificial and fictitious beauty. "The beauty of Cambyses's dresses," said he, "is as deceitful, it seems, as the fair show of his professions of friendship." As to the golden bracelets and necklaces, the king looked upon them with contempt. He thought that they were intended for fetters and chains, and said that, however well they might answer among the effeminate Persians, they were wholly insufficient to confine such sinews as he had to deal with. The wine, however, he liked. He drank it with great pleasure, and told the Icthyophagi that it was the only article among all their presents that was worth receiving.

In return for the presents which Cambyses had sent him, the King of the Ethiopians, who was a man of prodigious size and strength, took down his bow and gave it to the Icthyophagi, telling them to carry it to Cambyses as a token of his defiance, and to ask him to see if he could find a man in all his army who could bend it. "Tell Cambyses," he added, "that when his soldiers are able to bend such bows as that, it will be time for him to think of invading the territories of the Ethiopians; and that, in the mean time, he ought to consider himself very fortunate that the Ethiopians were not grasping and ambitious enough to attempt the invasion of his."

When the Icthyophagi returned to Cambyses with this message, the strongest men in the Persian camp were of course greatly interested in examining and trying the bow. Smerdis was the only one that could be found who was strong enough to bend it; and he, by the superiority to the others which he thus evinced, gained great renown. Cambyses was filled with jealousy and anger. He determined to send Smerdis back again to Persia. "It will be better," thought he to himself, "to incur whatever danger there may be of his exciting revolt at home, than to have him present in my court, subjecting me to continual mortification and chagrin by the perpetual parade of his superiority."

His mind was, however, not at ease after his brother had gone. Jealousy and suspicion in respect to Smerdis perplexed his waking thoughts and troubled his dreams. At length, one night, he thought he saw Smerdis seated on a royal throne in Persia, his form expanded supernaturally to such a prodigious size that he touched the heavens with his head. The next day, Cambyses, supposing that the dream portended danger that Smerdis would be one day in possession of the throne, determined to put a final and perpetual end to all these troubles and fears, and he sent for an officer of his court, Prexaspes--the same whose son he shot through the heart with an arrow, as described in the last chapter--and commanded him to proceed immediately to Persia, and there to find Smerdis, and kill him. The murder of Prexaspes's son, though related in the last chapter as an illustration of Cambyses's character, did not actually take place till after Prexaspes returned from this expedition.

Prexaspes went to Persia, and executed the orders of the king by the assassination of Smerdis. There are different accounts of the mode which he adopted for accomplishing his purpose. One is, that he contrived some way to drown him in the sea; another, that he poisoned him; and a third, that he killed him in the forests, when he was out on a hunting excursion. At all events, the deed was done, and Prexaspes went back to Cambyses, and reported to him that he had nothing further to fear from his brother's ambition.

In the mean time, Cambyses went on from bad to worse in his government, growing every day more despotic and tyrannical, and abandoning himself to fits of cruelty and passion which became more and more excessive and insane. At one time, on some slight provocation, he ordered twelve distinguished noblemen of his court to be buried alive. It is astonishing that there can be institutions and arrangements in the social state which will give one man such an ascendency over others that such commands can be obeyed. On another occasion, Cambyses's sister and wife, who had mourned the death of her brother Smerdis, ventured a reproach to Cambyses for having destroyed him. She was sitting at table, with some plant or flower in her hand, which she slowly picked to pieces, putting the fragments on the table. She asked Cambyses whether he thought the flower looked fairest and best in fragments, or in its original and natural integrity. "It looked best, certainly," Cambyses said, "when it was whole." "And yet," said she, "you have begun to take to pieces and destroy our family, as I have destroyed this flower." Cambyses sprang upon his unhappy sister, on hearing this reproof, with the ferocity of a tiger. He threw her down and leaped upon her. The attendants succeeded in rescuing her and bearing her away; but she had received a fatal injury. She fell immediately into a premature and unnatural sickness, and died.

These fits of sudden and terrible passion to which Cambyses was subject, were often followed, when they had passed by, as is usual in such cases, with remorse and misery; and sometimes the officers of Cambyses, anticipating a change in their master's feelings, did not execute his cruel orders, but concealed the object of his blind and insensate vengeance until the paroxysm was over. They did this once in the case of Croesus. Croesus, who was now a venerable man, advanced in years, had been for a long time the friend and faithful counselor of Cambyses's father. He had known Cambyses himself from his boyhood, and had been charged by his father to watch over him and counsel him, and aid him, on all occasions which might require it, with his experience and wisdom. Cambyses, too, had been solemnly charged by his father Cyrus, at the last interview that he had with him before his death, to guard and protect Croesus, as his father's ancient and faithful friend, and to treat him, as long as he lived, with the highest consideration and honor.

Under these circumstances, Croesus considered himself justified in remonstrating one day with Cambyses against his excesses and his cruelty. He told him that he ought not to give himself up to the control of such violent and impetuous passions; that, though his Persian soldiers and subjects had borne with him thus far, he might, by excessive oppression and cruelty, exhaust their forbearance and provoke them to revolt against him, and that thus he might suddenly lose his power, through his intemperate and inconsiderate use of it. Croesus apologized for offering these counsels, saying that he felt bound to warn Cambyses of his danger, in obedience to the injunctions of Cyrus, his father.

Cambyses fell into a violent passion at hearing these words. He told Croesus that he was amazed at his presumption in daring to offer him advice, and then began to load his venerable counselor with the bitterest invectives and reproaches. He taunted him with his own misfortunes, in losing, as he had done, years before, his own kingdom of Lydia, and then accused him of having been the means, through his foolish counsels, of leading his father, Cyrus, into the worst of the difficulties which befell him toward the close of his life. At last, becoming more and more enraged by the reaction upon himself of his own angry utterance, he told Croesus that he had hated him for a long time, and for a long time had wished to punish him; "and now," said he, "you have given me an opportunity." So saying, he seized his bow, and began to fit an arrow to the string. Croesus fled. Cambyses ordered his attendants to pursue him, and when they had taken him, to kill him. The officers knew that Cambyses would regret his rash and reckless command as soon as his anger should have subsided, and so, instead of slaying Croesus, they concealed him. A few days after, when the tyrant began to express his remorse and sorrow at having destroyed his venerable friend in the heat of passion, and to mourn his death, they told him that Croesus was still alive. They had ventured, they said, to save him, till they could ascertain whether it was the king's real and deliberate determination that he must die. The king was overjoyed to find Croesus still alive, but he would not forgive those who had been instrumental in saving him. He ordered every one of them to be executed.

Cambyses was the more reckless and desperate in these tyrannical cruelties because he believed that he possessed a sort of charmed life. He had consulted an oracle, it seems, in Media, in respect to his prospects of life, and the oracle had informed him that he would die at Ecbatane. Now Ecbatane was one of the three great capitals of his empire, Susa and Babylon being the others. Ecbatane was the most northerly of these cities, and the most remote from danger. Babylon and Susa were the points where the great transactions of government chiefly centered, while Ecbatane was more particularly the private residence of the kings. It was their refuge in danger, their retreat in sickness and age. In a word, Susa was their seat of government, Babylon their great commercial emporium, but Ecbatane was their home.

And thus as the oracle, when Cambyses inquired in respect to the circumstances of his death, had said that it was decreed by the fates that he should die at Ecbatane, it meant, as he supposed, that he should die in peace, in his bed, at the close of the usual period allotted to the life of man. Considering thus that the fates had removed all danger of a sudden and violent death from his path, he abandoned himself to his career of vice and folly, remembering only the substance of the oracle, while the particular form of words in which it was expressed passed from his mind.

At length Cambyses, after completing his conquests in Egypt, returned to the northward along the shores of the Mediterranean Sea, until he came into Syria. The province of Galilee, so often mentioned in the sacred Scriptures, was a part of Syria. In traversing Galilee at the head of the detachment of troops that was accompanying him, Cambyses came, one day, to a small town, and encamped there. The town itself was of so little importance that Cambyses did not, at the time of his arriving at it, even know its name. His encampment at the place, however, was marked by a very memorable event, namely, he met with a herald here, who was traveling through Syria, saying that he had been sent from Susa to proclaim to the people of Syria that Smerdis, the son of Cyrus, had assumed the throne, and to enjoin upon them all to obey no orders except such as should come from him!

Cambyses had supposed that Smerdis was dead. Prexaspes, when he had returned from Susa, had reported that he had killed him. He now, however, sent for Prexaspes, and demanded of him what this proclamation could mean. Prexaspes renewed, and insisted upon, his declaration that Smerdis was dead. He had destroyed him with his own hands, and had seen him buried. "If the dead can rise from the grave," added Prexaspes, "then Smerdis may perhaps, raise a revolt and appear against you; but not otherwise."

Prexaspes then recommended that the king should send and seize the herald, and inquire particularly of him in respect to the government in whose name he was acting. Cambyses did so. The herald was taken and brought before the king. On being questioned whether it was true that Smerdis had really assumed the government and commissioned him to make proclamation of the fact, he replied that it was so. He had not seen Smerdis himself, he said, for he kept himself shut up very closely in his palace; but he was informed of his accession by one of the magians whom Cambyses had left in command. It was by him, he said, that he had been commissioned to proclaim Smerdis as king.

Prexaspes then said that he had no doubt that the two magians whom Cambyses had left in charge of the government had contrived to seize the throne. He reminded Cambyses that the name of one of them was Smerdis, and that probably that was the Smerdis who was usurping the supreme command. Cambyses said that he was convinced that this supposition was true. His dream, in which he had seen a vision of Smerdis, with his head reaching to the heavens, referred, he had no doubt, to the magian Smerdis, and not to his brother. He began bitterly to reproach himself for having caused his innocent brother to be put to death; but the remorse which he thus felt for his crime, in assassinating an imaginary rival, soon gave way to rage and resentment against the real usurper. He called for his horse, and began to mount him in hot haste, to give immediate orders, and make immediate preparations for marching to Susa.

As he bounded into the saddle, with his mind in this state of reckless desperation, the sheath, by some accident or by some carelessness caused by his headlong haste, fell from his sword, and the naked point of the weapon pierced his thigh. The attendants took him from his horse, and conveyed him again to his tent. The wound, on examination, proved to be a very dangerous one, and the strong passions, the vexation, the disappointment, the impotent rage, which were agitating the mind of the patient, exerted an influence extremely unfavorable to recovery. Cambyses, terrified at the prospect of death, asked what was the name of the town where he was lying. They told him it was Ecbatane.

He had never thought before of the possibility that there might be some other Ecbatane besides his splendid royal retreat in Media; but now, when he learned that was the name of the place where he was then encamped, he felt sure that his hour was come, and he was overwhelmed with remorse and despair.

He suffered, too, inconceivable pain and anguish from his wound. The sword had pierced to the bone, and the inflammation which had supervened was of the worst character. After some days, the acuteness of the agony which he at first endured passed gradually away, though the extent of the injury resulting from the wound was growing every day greater and more hopeless. The sufferer lay, pale, emaciated, and wretched, on his couch, his mind, in every interval of bodily agony, filling up the void with the more dreadful sufferings of horror and despair.

At length, on the twentieth day after his wound had been received, he called the leading nobles of his court and officers of his army about his bedside, and said to them that he was about to die, and that he was compelled, by the calamity which had befallen him, to declare to them what he would otherwise have continued to keep concealed. The person who had usurped the throne under the name of Smerdis, he now said, was not, and could not be, his brother Smerdis, the son of Cyrus. He then proceeded to give them an account of the manner in which his fears in respect to his brother had been excited by his dream, and of the desperate remedy that he had resorted to in ordering him to be killed. He believed, he said, that the usurper was Smerdis the magian, whom he had left as one of the regents when he set out on his Egyptian campaign. He urged them, therefore, not to submit to his sway, but to go back to Media, and if they could not conquer him and put him down by open war, to destroy him by deceit and stratagem, or in any way whatever by which the end could be accomplished. Cambyses urged this with so much of the spirit of hatred and revenge beaming in his hollow and glassy eye as to show that sickness, pain, and the approach of death, which had made so total a change in the wretched sufferer's outward condition, had altered nothing within.

Very soon after making this communication to his nobles, Cambyses expired.

It will well illustrate the estimate which those who knew him best, formed of this great hero's character, to state, that those who heard this solemn declaration did not believe one word of it from beginning to end. They supposed that the whole story which the dying tyrant had told them, although he had scarcely breath enough left to tell it, was a fabrication, dictated by his fraternal jealousy and hate. They believed that it was really the true Smerdis who had been proclaimed king, and that Cambyses had invented, in his dying moments, the story of his having killed him, in order to prevent the Persians from submitting peaceably to his reign.

CHAPTER III.

SMERDIS THE MAGIAN.

Usurpation of the magians.--Circumstances favoring it.--Murder of Smerdis not known.--He is supposed to be alive.--Precautions taken by Smerdis.--Effect of Cambyses's measures.--Opinion in regard to Smerdis.--Acquiescence of the people.--Dangerous situation of Smerdis.--Arrangement with Patizithes.--Smerdis lives in retirement.--Special grounds of apprehension.--Cambyses's wives.--Smerdis appropriates them.--Phyma.--Measures of Otanes.--Otanes's communications with his daughter.--Her replies.--Phyma discovers the deception.--Otanes and the six nobles.--Arrival of Darius.--Secret consultations.--Various opinions.--Views of Darius.--Apology for a falsehood.--Opinion of Gobryas.--Uneasiness of the magi.--Situation of Prexaspes.--Measures of the magi.--An assembly of the people.--Decision of Prexaspes.--His speech from the tower.--Death of Prexaspes.--The conspirators.--The omen.--The conspirators enter the palace.--Combat with the magi.--Flight of Smerdis.--Smerdis is killed.--Exultation of the conspirators.--General massacre of the magians.

Cambyses and his friends had been right in their conjectures that it was Smerdis the magian who had usurped the Persian throne. This Smerdis resembled, it was said, the son of Cyrus in his personal appearance as well as in name. The other magian who had been associated with him in the regency when Cambyses set out from Persia on his Egyptian campaign was his brother. His name was Patizithes. When Cyrus had been some time absent, these magians, having in the mean time, perhaps, heard unfavorable accounts of his conduct and character, and knowing the effect which such wanton tyranny must have in alienating from him the allegiance of his subjects, conceived the design of taking possession of the empire in their own name. The great distance of Cambyses and his army from home, and his long-continued absence, favored this plan. Their own position, too, as they were already in possession of the capitals and the fortresses of the country, aided them; and then the name of Smerdis, being the same with that of the brother of Cambyses, was a circumstance that greatly promoted the success of the undertaking. In addition to all these general advantages, the cruelty of Cambyses was the means of furnishing them with a most opportune occasion for putting their plans into execution.

The reader will recollect that, as was related in the last chapter, Cambyses first sent his brother Smerdis home, and afterward, when alarmed by his dream, he sent Prexaspes to murder him. Now the return of Smerdis was publicly and generally known, while his assassination by Prexaspes was kept a profound secret. Even the Persians connected with Cambyses's court in Egypt had not heard of the perpetration of this crime, until Cambyses confessed it on his dying bed, and even then, as was stated in the last chapter, they did not believe it. It is not probable that it was known in Media and Persia; so that, after Prexaspes accomplished his work, and returned to Cambyses with the report of it, it was probably generally supposed that his brother was still alive, and was residing somewhere in one or another of the royal palaces.

Such royal personages were often accustomed to live thus, in a state of great seclusion, spending their time in effeminate pleasures within the walls of their palaces, parks, and gardens. When the royal Smerdis, therefore, secretly and suddenly disappeared, it would be very easy for the magian Smerdis, with the collusion of a moderate number of courtiers and attendants, to take his place, especially if he continued to live in retirement, and exhibited himself as little as possible to public view. Thus it was that Cambyses himself, by the very crimes which he committed to shield himself from all danger of a revolt, opened the way which specially invited it, and almost insured its success. Every particular step that he took, too, helped to promote the end. His sending Smerdis home; his waiting an interval, and then sending Prexaspes to destroy him; his ordering his assassination to be secret-- these, and all the other attendant circumstances, were only so many preliminary steps, preparing the way for the success of the revolution which was to accomplish his ruin. He was, in a word, his own destroyer. Like other wicked men, he found, in the end, that the schemes of wickedness which he had malignantly aimed at the destruction of others, had been all the time slowly and surely working out his own.

The people of Persia, therefore, were prepared by Cambyses's own acts to believe that the usurper Smerdis was really Cyrus's son, and, next to Cambyses, the heir to the throne. The army of Cambyses, too, in Egypt, believed the same. It was natural that they should do so for they placed no confidence whatever in Cambyses's dying declarations; and since intelligence, which seemed to be official, came from Susa declaring that Smerdis was still alive, and that he had actually taken possession of the throne, there was no apparent reason for doubting the fact. Besides, Prexaspes, as soon as

Cambyses was dead, considered it safer for him to deny than to confess having murdered the prince. He therefore declared that Cambyses's story was false, and that he had no doubt that Smerdis, the monarch in whose name the government was administered at Susa, was the son of Cyrus, the true and rightful heir to the throne. Thus all parties throughout the empire acquiesced peaceably in what they supposed to be the legitimate succession.

In the mean time, the usurper had placed himself in an exceedingly dizzy and precarious situation, and one which it would require a great deal of address and skillful management to sustain. The plan arranged between himself and his brother for a division of the advantages which they had secured by their joint and common cunning was, that Smerdis was to enjoy the ease and pleasure, and Patizithes the substantial power of the royalty which they had so stealthily seized. This was the safest plan. Smerdis, by living secluded, and devoting himself to retired and private pleasures, was the more likely to escape public observation; while Patizithes, acting as his prime minister of state, could attend councils, issue orders, review troops, dispatch embassies, and perform all the other outward functions of supreme command, with safety as well as pleasure. Patizithes seems to have been, in fact, the soul of the whole plan. He was ambitious and aspiring in character, and if he could only himself enjoy the actual exercise of royal power, he was willing that his brother should enjoy the honor of possessing it. Patizithes, therefore, governed the realm, acting, however, in all that he did, in Smerdis's name.

Smerdis, on his part, was content to take possession of the palaces, the parks, and the gardens of Media and Persia, and to live in them in retired and quiet luxury and splendor. He appeared seldom in public, and then only under such circumstances as should not expose him to any close observation on the part of the spectators. His figure, air, and manner, and the general cast of his countenance, were very much like those of the prince whom he was attempting to personate. There was one mark, however, by which he thought that there was danger that he might be betrayed, and that was, his ears had been cut off. This had been done many years before, by command of Cyrus, on account of some offense of which he had been guilty. The marks of the mutilation could, indeed, on public occasions, be concealed by the turban, or helmet, or other head-dress which he wore; but in private there was great danger either that the loss of the ears, or the studied effort to conceal it, should be observed. Smerdis was, therefore, very careful to avoid being seen in private, by keeping himself closely secluded. He shut himself up in the apartments of his palace at Susa, within the citadel, and never invited the Persian nobles to visit him there.

Among the other means of luxury and pleasure which Smerdis found in the royal palaces, and which he appropriated to his own enjoyment, were Cambyses's wives. In those times, Oriental princes and potentates--as is, in fact, the case at the present day, in many Oriental countries--possessed a great number of wives, who were bound to them by different sorts of matrimonial ties, more or less permanent, and bringing them into relations more or less intimate with their husband and sovereign. These wives were in many respects in the condition of slaves: in one particular they were especially so, namely, that on the death of a sovereign they descended, like any other property, to the heir, who added as many of them as he pleased to his own seraglio. Until this was done, the unfortunate women were shut up in close seclusion on the death of their lord, like mourners who retire from the world when suffering any great and severe bereavement.

The wives of Cambyses were appropriated by Smerdis to himself on his taking possession of the throne and hearing of Cambyses's death. Among them was Atossa, who has already been mentioned as the daughter of Cyrus, and, of course, the sister of Cambyses as well as his wife. In order to prevent these court ladies from being the means, in any way, of discovering the imposture which he was practicing, the magian continued to keep them all closely shut up in their several separate apartments, only allowing a favored few to visit him, one by one, in turn, while he prevented their having any communication with one another.

The name of one of these ladies was Phyma. She was the daughter of a Persian noble of the highest rank and influence, named Otanes. Otanes, as well as some other nobles of the court, had observed and reflected upon the extraordinary circumstances connected with the accession of Smerdis to the throne, and the singular mode of life that he led in secluding himself, in a manner so extraordinary for a Persian monarch, from all intercourse with his nobles and his people. The suspicions of Otanes and his associates were excited, but no one dared to communicate his thoughts to the others. At length, however, Otanes, who was a man of great energy as well as sagacity and discretion, resolved that he would take some measures to ascertain the truth.

He first sent a messenger to Phyma, his daughter, asking of her whether it was really Smerdis, the son of Cyrus, who received her when she went to visit the king. Phyma, in return, sent her father word that she did not know, for she had never seen Smerdis, the son of Cyrus, before the death of Cambyses. She therefore could not say, of her own personal knowledge, whether the king was the genuine Smerdis or not. Otanes then sent to Phyma a second time, requesting her to ask the queen Atossa. Atossa was the sister of Smerdis the prince, and had known him from his childhood. Phyma sent back word to her father that she could not speak to Atossa, for she was kept closely shut up in her own apartments, without the opportunity to communicate with any one. Otanes then sent a third time to his daughter, telling her that there was one remaining mode by which she might ascertain the truth, and that was, the next time that she visited the king, to feel for his ears when he was asleep. If it was Smerdis the magian, she would find that he had none. He urged his daughter to do this by saying that, if the pretended king was really an impostor, the imposture ought to be made known, and that she, being of noble birth, ought to have the courage and energy to assist in discovering it. To this Phyma replied that she would do as her father desired, though she knew that she hazarded her life in the attempt. "If he has no ears," said she, "and if I awaken him in attempting to feel for them, he will kill me; I am sure that he will kill me on the spot."

The next time that it came to Phyma's turn to visit the king, she did as her father had requested. She passed her hand very cautiously beneath the king's turban, and found that his ears had been cut off close to his head. Early in the morning she communicated the knowledge of the fact to her father.

Otanes immediately made the case known to two of his friends, Persian nobles, who had, with him, suspected the imposture, and had consulted together before in respect to the means of detecting it. The question was, what was now to be done. After some deliberation, it was agreed that each of them should communicate the discovery which they had made to one other person, such as each should select from among the circle of his friends as the one on whose resolution, prudence, and fidelity he could most implicitly rely. This was done, and the number admitted to the secret was thus increased to six. At this juncture it happened that Darius, the son of Hystaspes, the young man who has already been mentioned as the subject of Cyrus's dream, came to Susa. Darius was a man of great prominence and popularity. His father, Hystaspes, was at that time the governor of the province of Persia, and Darius had been residing with him in that country. As soon as the six conspirators heard of his arrival, they admitted him to their councils, and thus their number was increased to seven.

They immediately began to hold secret consultations for the purpose of determining how it was best to proceed, first binding themselves by the most solemn oaths never to betray one another, however their undertaking might end. Darius told them that he had himself discovered the imposture and usurpation of Smerdis, and that he had come from Persia for the purpose of slaying him; and that now, since it appeared that the secret was known to so many, he was of opinion that they ought to act at once with the utmost decision. He thought there would be great danger in delay.

Otanes, on the other hand, thought that they were not yet ready for action. They must first increase their numbers. Seven persons were too few to attempt to revolutionize an empire. He commended the courage and resolution which Darius displayed, but he thought that a more cautious and deliberate policy would be far more likely to conduct them to a safe result.

Darius replied that the course which Otanes recommended would certainly ruin them. "If we make many other persons acquainted with our plans," said he, "there will be some, notwithstanding all our precautions, who will betray us, for the sake of the immense rewards which they well know they would receive in that case from the king. No," he added, "we must act ourselves, and alone. We must do nothing to excite suspicion, but must go at once into the palace, penetrate boldly into Smerdis's presence, and slay him before he has time to suspect our designs."

"But we can not get into his presence," replied Otanes. "There are guards stationed at every gate and door, who will not allow us to pass. If we attempt to kill them, a tumult will be immediately raised, and the alarm given, and all our designs will thus be baffled."

"There will be little difficulty about the guards," said Darius. "They know us all, and, from deference to our rank and station, they will let us pass without suspicion, especially if we act boldly and promptly, and do not give them time to stop and consider what to do. Besides, I can say that I have just arrived from Persia with important dispatches for the king, and that I must be admitted immediately into his presence. If a falsehood must be told, so let it be. The urgency of the crisis demands and sanctions it."

It may seem strange to the reader, considering the ideas and habits of the times, that Darius should have even thought it necessary to apologize to his confederates for his proposal of employing falsehood in the accomplishment of their plans; and it is, in fact, altogether probable that the apology which he is made to utter is his historian's, and not his own.

The other conspirators had remained silent during this discussion between Darius and Otanes; but now a third, whose name was Gobryas, expressed his opinion in favor of the course which Darius recommended. He was aware, he said, that, in attempting to force their way into the king's presence and kill him by a sudden assault, they exposed themselves to the most imminent danger; but it was better for them to die in the manly attempt to bring back the imperial power again into Persian hands, where it properly belonged, than to acquiesce any further in its continuance in the possession of the ignoble Median priests who had so treacherously usurped it.

To this counsel they all finally agreed, and began to make arrangements for carrying their desperate enterprise into execution.

In the mean time, very extraordinary events were transpiring in another part of the city. The two magi, Smerdis the king and Patizithes his brother, had some cause, it seems, to fear that the nobles about the court, and the officers of the Persian army, were not without suspicions that the reigning monarch was not the real son of Cyrus. Rumors that Smerdis had been killed by Prexaspes, at the command of Cambyses, were in circulation. These rumors were contradicted, it is true, in private, by Prexaspes, whenever he was forced to speak of the subject; but he generally avoided it; and he spoke, when he spoke at all, in that timid and undecided tone which men usually assume when they are persisting in a lie. In the mean time, the gloomy recollections of his past life, the memory of his murdered son, remorse for his own crime in the assassination of Smerdis, and anxiety on account of the extremely dangerous position in which he had placed himself by his false denial of it, all conspired to harass his mind with perpetual restlessness and misery, and to make life a burden.

In order to do something to quiet the suspicions which the magi feared were prevailing, they did not know how extensively, they conceived the plan of inducing Prexaspes to declare in a more public and formal manner what he had been asserting timidly in private, namely, that Smerdis had not been killed. They accordingly convened an assembly of the people in a court-yard of the palace, or perhaps took advantage of some gathering casually convened, and proposed that Prexaspes should address them from a neighboring tower. Prexaspes was a man of high rank and of great influence, and the magi thought that his public espousal of their cause, and his open and decided contradiction of the rumor that he had killed Cambyses's brother, would fully convince the Persians that it was really the rightful monarch that had taken possession of the throne.

But the strength even of a strong man, when he has a lie to carry, soon becomes very small. That of Prexaspes was already almost exhausted and gone. He had been wavering and hesitating before, and this proposal, that he should commit himself so formally and solemnly, and in so public a manner, to statements wholly and absolutely untrue, brought him to a stand. He decided, desperately, in his own mind, that he would go on in his course of falsehood, remorse, and wretchedness no longer. He, however, pretended to accede to the propositions of the magi. He ascended the tower, and began to address the people. Instead, however, of denying that he had murdered Smerdis, he fully confessed to the astonished audience that he had really committed that crime; he openly denounced the reigning Smerdis as an impostor, and called upon all who heard him to rise at once, destroy the treacherous usurper, and vindicate the rights of the true Persian line. As he went on, with vehement voice and gestures, in this speech, the utterance of which he knew sealed his own destruction, he became more and more excited and reckless. He denounced his hearers in the severest language if they failed to obey his injunctions, and imprecated upon them, in that event, all the curses of Heaven. The people listened to this strange and sudden phrensy of eloquence in utter amazement, motionless and silent; and before they or the officers of the king's household who were present had time even to consider what to do, Prexaspes, coming abruptly to the conclusion of his harangue, threw himself headlong from the parapet of the tower, and came down among them, lifeless and mangled, on the pavement below.

Of course, all was now tumult and commotion in the court-yard, and it happened to be just at this juncture that the seven conspirators came from the place of their consultation to the palace, with a view of executing their plans. They were soon informed of what had taken place. Otanes was now again disposed to postpone their attempt upon the life of the king. The event which had occurred changed, he said, the aspect of the subject, and they must wait until the tumult and excitement should have somewhat subsided. But Darius was more eager than ever in favor of instantaneous action. He said that there was not a moment to be lost; for the magi, so soon as they should be informed of the declarations and of the death of Prexaspes, would be alarmed, and would take at once the most effectual precautions to guard against any sudden assault or surprise.

These arguments, at the very time in which Darius was offering them with so much vehemence and earnestness, were strengthened by a very singular sort of confirmation; for while the conspirators stood undetermined, they saw a flock of birds moving across the sky, which, on their more attentively regarding them, proved to be seven hawks pursuing two vultures. This they regarded an omen, intended to signify to them, by a divine intimation, that they ought to proceed. They hesitated, therefore, no longer.

They went together to the outer gates of the palace. The action of the guards who were stationed there was just what Darius had predicted that it would be. Awed by the imposing spectacle of the approach of seven nobles of the highest distinction, who were advancing, too, with an earnest and confident air, as if expecting no obstacle to their admission, they gave way at once, and allowed them to enter. The conspirators went on until they came to the inner apartments, where they found eunuchs in attendance at the doors. The eunuchs resisted, and demanded angrily why the guards had let the strangers in. "Kill them," said the conspirators, and immediately began to cut them down. The magi were within, already in consternation at the disclosures of Prexaspes, of which they had just been informed. They heard the tumult and the outcries of the eunuchs at the doors, and seized their arms, the one a bow and the other a spear. The conspirators rushed in. The bow was useless in the close combat which ensued, and the magian who had taken it turned and fled. The other defended himself with his spear for a moment, and wounded severely two of his assailants. The wounded conspirators fell. Three others of the number continued the unequal combat with the armed magian, while Darius and Gobryas rushed in pursuit of the other.

The flying magian ran from one apartment to another until he reached a dark room, into which the blind instinct of fear prompted him to rush, in the vain hope of concealment. Gobryas was foremost; he seized the wretched fugitive by the waist, and struggled to hold him, while the magian struggled to get free. Gobryas called upon Darius, who was close behind him, to strike. Darius, brandishing his sword, looked earnestly into the obscure retreat, that he might see where to strike.

"Strike!" exclaimed Gobryas. "Why do you not strike?"

"I can not see," said Darius, "and I am afraid of wounding you."

"No matter," said Gobryas, struggling desperately all the time with his frantic victim. "Strike quick, if you kill us both."

Darius struck. Gobryas loosened his hold, and the magian fell upon the floor, and there, stabbed again through the heart by Darius's sword, almost immediately ceased to breathe.

They dragged the body to the light, and cut off the head. They did the same with the other magian, whom they found that their confederates had killed when they returned to the apartments where they had left them contending. The whole body of the conspirators then, except the two who were wounded, exulting in their success, and wild with the excitement which such deeds always awaken, went forth into the streets of the city, bearing the heads upon pikes as the trophies of their victory. They summoned the Persian soldiers to arms, and announced every where that they had ascertained that the king was a priest and an impostor, and not their legitimate sovereign, and that they had consequently killed him. They called upon the people to kill the magians wherever they could find them, as if the whole class were implicated in the guilt of the usurping brothers.

The populace in all countries are easily excited by such denunciations and appeals as these. The Persians armed themselves, and ran to and fro every where in pursuit of the unhappy magians, and before night vast numbers of them were slain.

CHAPTER IV.

THE ACCESSION OF DARIUS.

B.C. 520

Confusion at Susa.--No heir to the throne.--Five days' interregnum.--Provisional government.--Consultation of the confederates.--Otanes in favor of a republic.--Otanes's republic.--Principles of representation.--Large assemblies.--Nature of ancient republics.--Nature of a representative republic.--Megabyzus.--He opposes the plan of Otanes.--Speech of Megabyzus.--He proposes an oligarchy.--Speech of Darius.--He advocates a monarchy.--Four of the seven confederates concur with Darius.--Otanes withdraws.--Agreement made by the rest.--Singular mode of deciding which should be the king.--The groom Oebases.--His method of making Darius's horse neigh.--Probable truth or falsehood of this account.--Ancient statesmen.--Their character and position.--The conspirators governed, in their decision, by superstitious feelings.--The conspirators do homage to Darius.--The equestrian statue.

For several days after the assassination of the magi the city was filled with excitement, tumults, and confusion. There was no heir, of the family of Cyrus, entitled to succeed to the vacant throne, for neither Cambyses, nor Smerdis his brother, had left any sons. There was, indeed, a daughter of Smerdis, named Parmys, and there were also still living two daughters of Cyrus. One was Atossa, whom we have already mentioned as having been married to Cambyses, her brother, and as having been afterward taken by Smerdis the magian as one of his wives. These princesses, though of royal lineage, seem neither of them to have been disposed to assert any claims to the throne at such a crisis. The mass of the community were stupefied with astonishment at the sudden revolution which had occurred. No movement was made toward determining the succession. For five days nothing was done.

During this period, all the subordinate functions of government in the provinces, cities, and towns, and among the various garrisons and encampments of the army, went on, of course, as usual, but the general administration of the government had no head. The seven confederates had been regarded, for the time being, as a sort of provisional government, the army and the country in general, so far as appears, looking to them for the means of extrication from the political difficulties in which this sudden revolution had involved them, and submitting, in the mean time, to their direction and control. Such a state of things, it was obvious, could not long last; and after five days, when the commotion had somewhat subsided, they began to consider it necessary to make some arrangements of a more permanent character, the power to make such arrangements as they thought best resting with them alone. They accordingly met for consultation.

Herodotus the historian,[C] on whose narrative of these events we have mainly to rely for all the information respecting them which is now to be attained, gives a very minute and dramatic account of the deliberations of the conspirators on this occasion. The account is, in fact, too dramatic to be probably true.

[Footnote C: An account of Herodotus, and of the circumstances under which he wrote his history, which will aid the reader very much in forming an opinion in respect to the kind and degree of confidence which it is proper to place in his statements, will be found in the first chapter of our history of Cyrus the Great.]

Otanes, in this discussion, was in favor of establishing a republic. He did not think it safe or wise to intrust the supreme power again to any single individual. It was proved, he said, by universal experience, that when any one person was raised to such an elevation above his fellow-men, he became suspicious, jealous, insolent, and cruel. He lost all regard for the welfare and happiness of others, and became supremely devoted to the preservation of his own greatness and power by any means, however tyrannical, and to the accomplishment of the purposes of his own despotic will. The best and most valuable citizens were as likely to become the victims of his oppression as the worst. In fact, tyrants generally chose their favorites, he said, from among the most abandoned men and women in their realms, such characters being the readiest instruments of their guilty pleasures and their crimes. Otanes referred very particularly to the case of Cambyses as an example of the extreme lengths to which the despotic insolence and cruelty of a tyrant could go. He reminded his colleagues of the sufferings and terrors which they had endured while under his sway, and urged them very strongly not to expose themselves to such terrible evils and dangers again. He proposed, therefore, that they should establish a republic, under which the officers of government should be elected, and questions of public policy be determined, in assemblies of the people.

It must be understood, however, by the reader, that a republic, as contemplated and intended by Otanes in this speech, was entirely different from the mode of government which that word denotes at the present day. They had little idea, in those times, of the principle of representation, by which the thousand separate and detached communities of a great empire can choose delegates, who are to deliberate, speak, and act for them in the assemblies where the great governmental decisions are ultimately made. By this principle of representation, the people can really all share in the exercise of power. Without it they can not, for it is impossible that the people of a great state can ever be brought together in one assembly; nor, even if it were practicable to bring them thus together, would it be possible for such a concourse to deliberate or act. The action of any assembly which goes beyond a very few hundred in numbers, is always, in fact, the action exclusively of the small knot of leaders who call and manage it. Otanes, therefore, as well as all other advocates of republican government in ancient times, meant that the supreme power should be exercised, not by the great mass of the people included within the jurisdiction in question, but by such a portion of certain privileged classes as could be brought together in the capital. It was such a sort of republic as would be formed in this country if the affairs of the country at large, and the municipal and domestic institutions of all the states, were regulated and controlled by laws enacted, and by governors appointed, at great municipal meetings held in the city of New York.

This was, in fact, the nature of all the republics of ancient times. They were generally small, and the city in whose free citizens the supreme power resided, constituted by far the most important portion of the body politic. The Roman republic, however, became at one period very large. It overspread almost the whole of Europe; but, widely extended as it was in territory, and comprising innumerable states and kingdoms within its jurisdiction, the vast concentration of power by which the whole was governed, vested entirely and exclusively in noisy and tumultuous assemblies convened in the Roman forum.

Even if the idea of a representative system of government, such as is adopted in modern times, and by means of which the people of a great and extended empire can exercise, conveniently and efficiently, a general sovereignty held in common by them all, had been understood in ancient times, it is very doubtful whether it could, in those times, have been carried into effect, for want of certain facilities which are enjoyed in the present age, and which seem essential for the safe and easy action of so vast and complicated a system as a great representative government must necessarily be. The regular transaction of business at public meetings, and the orderly and successful management of any extended system of elections, requires a great deal of writing; and the general circulation of newspapers, or something exercising the great function which it is the object of newspapers to fulfill, that of keeping the people at large in some degree informed in respect to the progress of public affairs, seems essential to the successful working of a system of representative government comprising any considerable extent of territory.

However this may be, whether a great representative system would or would not have been practicable in ancient times if it had been tried, it is certain that it was never tried. In all ancient republics, the sovereignty resided, essentially, in a privileged class of the people of the capital. The territories governed were provinces, held in subjection as dependencies, and compelled to pay tribute; and this was the plan which Otanes meant to advocate when recommending a republic, in the Persian council.

The name of the second speaker in this celebrated consultation was Megabyzus. He opposed the plan of Otanes. He concurred fully, he said, in all that Otanes had advanced in respect to the evils of a monarchy, and to the oppression and tyranny to which a people were exposed whose liberties and lives were subject to the despotic control of a single human will. But in order to avoid one extreme, it was not necessary to run into the evils of the other. The disadvantages and dangers of popular control in the management of the affairs of state were scarcely less than those of a despotism. Popular assemblies were always, he said, turbulent, passionate, capricious. Their decisions were controlled by artful and designing demagogues. It was not possible that masses of the common people could have either the sagacity to form wise counsels, or the energy and steadiness to execute them. There could be no deliberation, no calmness, no secrecy in their consultations. A populace was always governed by excitements, which spread among them by a common sympathy; and they would give way impetuously to the most senseless impulses, as they were urged by their fear, their resentment, their exultation, their hate, or by any other passing emotion of the hour.

Megabyzus therefore disapproved of both a monarchy and a republic. He recommended an oligarchy. "We are now," said he, "already seven. Let us select from the leading nobles in the court and officers of the army a small number of men, eminent for talents and virtue, and thus form a select and competent body of men, which shall be the depository of the supreme power. Such a plan avoids the evils and inconveniences of both the other systems. There can be no tyranny or oppression under such a system; for, if any one of so large a number should be inclined to abuse his power, he will be restrained by the rest. On the other hand, the number will not be so large as to preclude prudence and deliberation in counsel, and the highest efficiency and energy in carrying counsels into effect."

When Megabyzus had completed his speech, Darius expressed his opinion. He said that the arguments of those who had already spoken appeared plausible, but that the speakers had not dealt quite fairly by the different systems whose merits they had discussed, since they had compared a good administration of one form of government with a bad administration of another. Every thing human was, he admitted, subject to imperfection and liable to abuse; but on the supposition that each of the three forms which had been proposed were equally well administered, the advantage, he thought, would be strongly on the side of monarchy. Control exercised by a single mind and will was far more concentrated and efficient than that proceeding from any conceivable combination. The forming of plans could be, in that case, more secret and wary, and the execution of them more immediate and prompt. Where power was lodged in many hands, all energetic exercise of it was paralyzed by the dissensions, the animosities and the contending struggles of envious and jealous rivals. These struggles, in fact, usually resulted in the predominance of some one, more energetic or more successful than the rest, the aristocracy or the democracy running thus, of its own accord, to a despotism in the end, showing that there were natural causes always tending to the subjection of nations of men to the control of one single will.

Besides all this, Darius added, in conclusion, that the Persians had always been accustomed to a monarchy, and it would be a very dangerous experiment to attempt to introduce a new system, which would require so great a change in all the habits and usages of the people.

Thus the consultation went on. At the end of it, it appeared that four out of the seven agreed with Darius in preferring a monarchy. This was a majority, and thus the question seemed to be settled. Otanes said that he would make no opposition to any measures which they might adopt to carry their decision into effect, but that he would not himself be subject to the monarchy which they might establish. "I do not wish," he added, "either to govern others or to have others govern me. You may establish a kingdom, therefore, if you choose, and designate the monarch in any mode that you see fit to adopt, but he must not consider me as one of his subjects. I myself, and all my family and dependents, must be wholly free from his control."

This was a very unreasonable proposition, unless, indeed, Otanes was willing to withdraw altogether from the community to which he thus refused to be subject; for, by residing within it, he necessarily enjoyed its protection, and ought, therefore, to bear his portion of its burdens, and to be amenable to its laws. Notwithstanding this, however, the conspirators acceded to the proposal, and Otanes withdrew.

The remaining six of the confederates then proceeded with their arrangements for the establishment of a monarchy. They first agreed that one of their own number should be the king, and that on whomsoever the choice should fall, the other five, while they submitted to his dominion, should always enjoy peculiar privileges and honors at his court. They were at all times to have free access to the palaces and to the presence of the king, and it was from among their daughters alone that the king was to choose his wives. These and some other similar points having been arranged, the manner of deciding which of the six should be the king remained to be determined. The plan which they adopted, and the circumstances connected with the execution of it, constitute, certainly, one of the most extraordinary of all the strange transactions recorded in ancient times. It is gravely related by Herodotus as sober truth. How far it is to be considered as by any possibility credible, the reader must judge, after knowing what the story is.

They agreed, then, that on the following morning they would all meet on horseback at a place agreed upon beyond the walls of the city, and that the one whose horse should neigh first should be the king! The time when this ridiculous ceremony was to be performed was sunrise.

As soon as this arrangement was made the parties separated, and each went to his own home. Darius called his groom, whose name was OEbases, and ordered him to have his horse ready at sunrise on the next morning, explaining to him, at the same time, the plan which had been formed for electing the king. "If that is the mode which is to be adopted," said Oebases, "you need have no concern, for I can arrange it very easily so as to have the lot fall upon you." Darius expressed a strong desire to have this accomplished, if it were possible, and Oebases went away.

The method which Oebases adopted was to lead Darius's horse out to the ground that evening, in company with another, the favorite companion, it seems, of the animal. Now the attachment of the horse to his companion is very strong, and his recollection of localities very vivid, and Oebases expected that when the horse should approach the ground on the following morning, he would be reminded of the company which he enjoyed there the night before, and neigh. The result was as he anticipated. As the horsemen rode up to the appointed place, the horse of Darius neighed the first, and Darius was unanimously acknowledged king.

In respect to the credibility of this famous story, the first thought which arises in the mind is, that it is utterly impossible that sane men, acting in so momentous a crisis, and where interests so vast and extended were at stake, could have resorted to a plan so childish and ridiculous as this. Such a mode of designating a leader, seriously adopted, would have done discredit to a troop of boys making arrangements for a holiday; and yet here was an empire extending for thousands of miles through the heart of a vast continent, comprising, probably, fifty nations and many millions of people, with capitals, palaces, armies, fleets, and all the other appointments and machinery of an immense dominion, to be appropriated and disposed of absolutely, and, so far as they could see, forever. It seems incredible that men possessing such intelligence, and information, and extent of view as we should suppose that officers of their rank and station would necessarily acquire, could have attempted to decide such a momentous question in so ridiculous and trivial a manner. And yet the account is seriously recorded by Herodotus as sober history, and the story has been related again and again, from that day to this, by every successive generation of historians, without any particular question of its truth.

And it may possibly be that it is true. It is a case in which the apparent improbability is far greater than the real. In the first place, it would seem that, in all ages of the world, the acts and decisions of men occupying positions of the most absolute and exalted power have been controlled, to a much greater degree, by caprice and by momentary impulse, than mankind have generally supposed. Looking up as we do to these vast elevations from below, they seem invested with a certain sublimity and grandeur which we imagine must continually impress the minds of those who occupy them, and expand and strengthen their powers, and lead them to act, in all respects, with the circumspection, the deliberation, and the far-reaching sagacity which the emergencies continually arising seem to require. And this is, in fact, in some degree the case with the statesmen and political leaders raised to power under the constitutional governments of modern times. Such statesmen are clothed with their high authority, in one way or another, by the combined and deliberate action of vast masses of men, and every step which they take is watched, in reference to its influence on the condition and welfare of these masses, by many millions; so that such men live and act under a continual sense of responsibility, and they appreciate, in some degree, the momentous importance of their doings. But the absolute and independent sovereigns of the Old World, who held their power by conquest or by inheritance, though raised sometimes to very vast and giddy elevations, seem to have been unconscious, in many instances, of the dignity and grandeur of their standing, and to have considered their acts only as they affected their own personal and temporary interests. Thus, though placed on a great elevation, they took only very narrow and circumscribed views; they saw nothing but the objects immediately around them; and they often acted, accordingly, in the most frivolous and capricious manner.

It was so, undoubtedly, with these six conspirators. In deciding which of their number should be king, they thought nothing of the interests of the vast realms, and of the countless millions of people whose government was to be provided for. The question, as they considered it, was doubtless merely which of them should have possession of the royal palaces, and be the center and the object of royal pomp and parade in the festivities and celebrations of the capital.

And in the mode of decision which they adopted, it may be that some degree of superstitious feeling mingled. The action and the voices of animals were considered, in those days, as supernatural omens, indicating the will of heaven. These conspirators may have expected, accordingly, in the neighing of the horse, a sort of divine intimation in respect to the disposition of the crown. This idea is confirmed by the statement which the account of this transaction contains, that immediately after the neighing of Darius's horse, it thundered, although there were no clouds in the sky from which the thunder could be supposed naturally to come. The conspirators, at all events, considered it solemnly decided that Darius was to be king. They all dismounted from their horses and knelt around him, in acknowledgment of their allegiance and subjection.

It seems that Darius, after he became established on his throne, considered the contrivance by which, through the assistance of his groom, he had obtained the prize, not as an act of fraud which it was incumbent on him to conceal, but as one of brilliant sagacity which he was to avow and glory in. He caused a magnificent equestrian statue to be sculptured, representing himself mounted on his neighing horse. This statue he set up in a public place with this inscription:

DARIUS, SON OF HYSTASPES, OBTAINED THE SOVEREIGNTY OF PERSIA BY THE SAGACITY OF HIS HORSE AND THE INGENIOUS CONTRIVANCE OF OEBASES HIS GROOM.

CHAPTER V.

THE PROVINCES.

B.C. 520

Several of the events and incidents which occurred immediately after the accession of Darius to the throne, illustrate in a striking manner the degree in which the princes and potentates of ancient days were governed by caprice and passionate impulse even in their public acts. One of the most remarkable of these was the case of Intaphernes.

Intaphernes was one of the seven conspirators who combined to depose the magian and place Darius on the throne. By the agreement which they made with each other before it was decided which should be the king, each of them was to have free access to the king's presence at all times. One evening, soon after Darius became established on his throne, Intaphernes went to the palace, and was proceeding to enter the apartment of the king without ceremony, when he was stopped by two officers, who told him that the king had retired. Intaphernes was incensed at the officers' insolence, as he called it. He drew his sword, and cut off their noses and their ears. Then he took the bridle off from his horse at the palace gate, and tied the officers together; and then, leaving them in this helpless and miserable condition, he went away.

The officers immediately repaired to the king, and presented themselves to him, a frightful spectacle, wounded and bleeding, and complaining bitterly of Intaphernes as the author of the injuries which they had received. The king was at first alarmed for his own safety. He feared that the conspirators had all combined together to rebel against his authority, and that this daring insult offered to his personal attendants, in his very palace, was the first outbreak of it. He accordingly sent for the conspirators one by one, to ask of them whether they approved of what Intaphernes had done. They promptly disavowed all connection with Intaphernes in the act, and all approval of it, and declared their determination to adhere to the decision that they had made, by which Darius had been placed on the throne.

Darius then, after taking proper precautions to guard against any possible attempts at resistance, sent soldiers to seize Intaphernes, and also his son, and all of his family, relatives, and friends who were capable of bearing arms; for he suspected that Intaphernes had meditated a rebellion, and he thought that, if so, these men would most probably be his accomplices. The prisoners were brought before him. There was, indeed, no proof that they were engaged in any plan of rebellion, nor even that any plan of rebellion whatever had been formed; but this circumstance afforded them no protection. The liberties and the lives of all subjects were at the supreme and absolute disposal of these ancient kings. Darius thought it possible that the prisoners had entertained, or might entertain, some treasonable designs, and he conceived that he should, accordingly, feel safer if they were removed out of the way. He decreed, therefore, that they must all die.

While the preparations were making for the execution, the wife of Intaphernes came continually to the palace of Darius, begging for an audience, that she might intercede for the lives of her friends. Darius was informed of this, and at last, pretending to be moved with compassion for her distress, he sent her word that he would pardon one of the criminals for her sake, and that she might decide which one it should be. His real motive in making this proposal seems to have been to enjoy the perplexity and anguish which the heart of a woman must suffer in being compelled thus to decide, in a question of life and death, between a husband and a son.

The wife of Intaphernes did not decide in favor of either of these. She gave the preference, on the other hand, to a brother. Darius was very much surprised at this result, and sent a messenger to her to inquire how it happened that she could pass over and abandon to their fate her husband and her son, in order to save the life of her brother, who was certainly to be presumed less near and dear to her. To which she gave this extraordinary reply, that the loss of her husband and her son might perhaps be repaired, since it was not impossible that she might be married again, and that she might have another son; but that, inasmuch as both her father and mother were dead, she could never have another brother. The death of her present brother would, therefore, be an irreparable loss.

The king was so much pleased with the novelty and unexpectedness of this turn of thought, that he gave her the life of her son in addition to that of her brother. All the rest of the family circle of relatives and friends, together with Intaphernes himself, he ordered to be slain.

Darius had occasion to be so much displeased, too, shortly after his accession to the throne, with the governor of one of his provinces, that he was induced to order him to be put to death. The circumstances connected with this governor's crime, and the manner of his execution, illustrate very forcibly the kind of government which was administered by these military despots in ancient times. It must be premised that great empires, like that over which Darius had been called to rule, were generally divided into provinces. The inhabitants of these provinces, each community within its own borders, went on, from year to year, in their various pursuits of peaceful industry, governed mainly, in their relations to each other, by the natural sense of justice instinctive in man, and by those thousand local institutions and usages which are always springing up in all human communities under the influence of this principle. There were governors stationed over these provinces, whose main duty it was to collect and remit to the king the tribute which the province was required to furnish him. These governors were, of course, also to suppress any domestic outbreak of violence, and to repel any foreign invasion which might occur. A sufficient military force was placed at their disposal to enable them to fulfill these functions. They paid these troops, of course, from sums which they collected in their provinces under the same system by which they collected the tribute. This made them, in a great measure, independent of the king in the maintenance of their armies. They thus intrenched themselves in their various capitals at the head of these troops, and reigned over their respective dominions almost as if they were kings themselves. They had, in fact, very little connection with the supreme monarch, except to send him the annual tribute which they had collected from their people, and to furnish, also, their quota of troops in case of a national war. In the time of our Savior, Pilate was such a governor, intrusted by the Romans with the charge of Judea, and Matthew was one of the tax gatherers employed to collect the tribute.

Of course, the governors of such provinces, as we have already said, were, in a great measure, independent of the king. He had, ordinarily, no officers of justice whose jurisdiction could control, peacefully, such powerful vassals. The only remedy in most cases, when they were disobedient and rebellious, was to raise an army and go forth to make war upon them, as in the case of any foreign state. This was attended with great expense, and trouble, and hazard. The governors, when ambitious and aspiring, sometimes managed their resources with so much energy and military skill as to get the victory over their sovereign in the contests in which they engaged with them, and then they would gain vast accessions to the privileges and powers which they exercised in their own departments; and they would sometimes overthrow their discomfited sovereign entirely, and take possession of his throne themselves in his stead.

Oretes was the name of one of these governors in the time of Darius. He had been placed by Cyrus, some years before, in charge of one of the provinces into which the kingdom of Lydia had been divided. The seat of government was Sardis.[D] He was a capricious and cruel tyrant, as, in fact, almost all such governors were. We will relate an account of one of the deeds which he performed some time before Darius ascended the throne, and which sufficiently illustrates his character.

[Footnote D: For the position of Sardis, and of other places mentioned in this chapter, see the map at the commencement of the volume, and also that at the commencement of chapter xi.]

He was one day sitting at the gates of his palace in Sardis, in conversation with the governor of a neighboring territory who had come to visit him. The name of this guest was Mitrobates. As the two friends were boasting to one another, as such warriors are accustomed to do, of the deeds of valor and prowess which they had respectively performed, Mitrobates said that Oretes could not make any great pretensions to enterprise and bravery so long as he allowed the Greek island of Samos, which was situate at a short distance from the Lydian coast, to remain independent, when it would be so easy to annex it to the Persian empire. "You are afraid of Polycrates, I suppose," said he. Polycrates was the king of Samos.

Oretes was stung by this taunt, but, instead of revenging himself on Mitrobates, the author of it, he resolved on destroying Polycrates, though he had no reason other than this for any feeling of enmity toward him.

Polycrates, although the seat of his dominion was a small island in the 茨 ean Sea, was a very wealthy, and powerful, and prosperous prince. All his plans and enterprises had been remarkably successful. He had built and equipped a powerful fleet, and had conquered many islands in the neighborhood of his own. He was projecting still wider schemes of conquests, and hoped, in fact, to make himself the master of all the seas.

A very curious incident is related of Polycrates, which illustrates very strikingly the childish superstition which governed the minds of men in those ancient days. It seems that in the midst of his prosperity, his friend and ally, the King of Egypt--for these events, though narrated here, occurred before the invasion of Egypt by Cambyses--sent to him a letter, of which the following is the purport.

"Amasis, king of Egypt, to Polycrates.

"It always gives me great satisfaction and pleasure to hear of the prosperity of a friend and ally, unless it is too absolutely continuous and uninterrupted. Something like an alternation of good and ill fortune is best for man; I have never known an instance of a very long-continued course of unmingled and uninterrupted success that did not end, at last, in overwhelming and terrible calamity. I am anxious, therefore, for you, and my anxiety will greatly increase if this extraordinary and unbroken prosperity should continue much longer. I counsel you, therefore, to break the current yourself, if fortune will not break it. Bring upon yourself some calamity, or loss, or suffering, as a means of averting the heavier evils which will otherwise inevitably befall you. It is a general and substantial welfare only that can be permanent and final."

Polycrates seemed to think there was good sense in this suggestion. He began to look around him to see in what way he could bring upon himself some moderate calamity or loss, and at length decided on the destruction of a very valuable signet ring which he kept among his treasures. The ring was made with very costly jewels set in gold, and was much celebrated both for its exquisite workmanship and also for its intrinsic value. The loss of this ring would be, he thought, a sufficient calamity to break the evil charm of an excessive and unvaried current of good fortune. Polycrates, therefore, ordered one of the largest vessels in his navy, a fifty-oared galley, to be equipped and manned, and, embarking in it with a large company of attendants, he put to sea. When he was at some distance from the island, he took the ring, and in the presence of all his attendants, he threw it forth into the water, and saw it sink, to rise, as he supposed, no more.

But Fortune, it seems, was not to be thus outgeneraled. A few days after Polycrates had returned, a certain fisherman on the coast took, in his nets, a fish of very extraordinary size and beauty; so extraordinary, in fact, that he felt it incumbent on him to make a present of it to the king. The servants of Polycrates, on opening the fish for the purpose of preparing it for the table, to their great astonishment and gratification, found the ring within. The king was overjoyed at thus recovering his lost treasure; he had, in fact, repented of his rashness in throwing it away, and had been bitterly lamenting its loss. His satisfaction and pleasure were, therefore, very great in regaining it; and he immediately sent to Amasis an account of the whole transaction, expecting that Amasis would share in his joy.

Amasis, however, sent word back to him in reply, that he considered the return of the ring in that almost miraculous manner as an extremely unfavorable omen. "I fear," said he, "that it is decreed by the Fates that you must be overwhelmed, at last, by some dreadful calamity, and that no measures of precaution which you can adopt will avail to avert it. It seems to me, too," he added, "that it is incumbent on me to withdraw from all alliance and connection with you, lest I should also, at last, be involved in your destined destruction."

Whether this extraordinary story was true, or whether it was all fabricated after the fall of Polycrates, as a dramatic embellishment of his history, we can not now know. The result, however, corresponded with these predictions of Amasis, if they were really made; for it was soon after these events that the conversation took place at Sardis between Oretes and Mitrobates, at the gates of the palace, which led Oretes to determine on effecting Polycrates's destruction.

In executing the plans which he thus formed, Oretes had not the courage and energy necessary for an open attack on Polycrates, and he consequently resolved on attempting to accomplish his end by treachery and stratagem.

The plan which he devised was this: He sent a messenger to Polycrates with a letter of the following purport:

"Oretes, governor of Sardis, to Polycrates of Samos.

"I am aware, sire, of the plans which you have long been entertaining for extending your power among the islands and over the waters of the Mediterranean, until you shall have acquired the supreme and absolute dominion of the seas. I should like to join you in this enterprise. You have ships and men, and I have money. Let us enter into an alliance with each other. I have accumulated in my treasuries a large supply of gold and silver, which I will furnish for the expenses of the undertaking. If you have any doubt of my sincerity in making these offers, and of my ability to fulfill them, send some messenger in whom you have confidence, and I will lay the evidence before him."

Polycrates was much pleased at the prospect of a large accession to his funds, and he sent the messenger, as Oretes had proposed. Oretes prepared to receive him by filling a large number of boxes nearly full with heavy stones, and then placing a shallow layer of gold or silver coin at the top. These boxes were then suitably covered and secured, with the fastenings usually adopted in those days, and placed away in the royal treasuries. When the messenger arrived, the boxes were brought out and opened, and were seen by the messenger to be full, as he supposed, of gold and silver treasure. The messenger went back to Polycrates, and reported that all which Oretes had said was true; and Polycrates then determined to go to the main land himself to pay Oretes a visit, that they might mature together their plans for the intended campaigns. He ordered a fifty-oared galley to be prepared to convey him.

His daughter felt a presentiment, it seems, that some calamity was impending. She earnestly entreated her father not to go. She had had a dream, she said, about him, which had frightened her excessively, and which she was convinced portended some terrible danger. Polycrates paid no attention to his daughter's warnings. She urged them more and more earnestly, until, at last, she made her father angry, and then she desisted. Polycrates then embarked on board his splendid galley, and sailed away. As soon as he landed in the dominions of Oretes, the monster seized him and put him to death, and then ordered his body to be nailed to a cross, for exhibition to all passers by, as a public spectacle. The train of attendants and servants that accompanied Polycrates on this expedition were all made slaves, except a few persons of distinction, who were sent home in a shameful and disgraceful manner. Among the attendants who were detained in captivity by Oretes was a celebrated family physician, named Democedes, whose remarkable and romantic adventures will be the subject of the next chapter.

Oretes committed several other murders and assassinations in this treacherous manner, without any just ground for provocation. In these deeds of violence and cruelty, he seems to have acted purely under the influence of that wanton and capricious malignity which the possession of absolute and irresponsible power so often engenders in the minds of bad men. It is doubtful, however, whether these cruelties and crimes would have particularly attracted the attention of Darius, so long as he was not himself directly affected by them. The central government, in these ancient empires, generally interested itself very little in the contentions and quarrels of the governors of the provinces, provided that the tribute was efficiently collected and regularly paid.

A case, however, soon occurred, in Oretes's treacherous and bloody career, which arrested the attention of Darius and aroused his ire. Darius had sent a messenger to Oretes, with certain orders, which, it seems, Oretes did not like to obey. After delivering his dispatches the bearer set out on his return, and was never afterward heard of. Darius ascertained, to his own satisfaction at least, that Oretes had caused his messenger to be waylaid and killed, and that the bodies both of horse and rider had been buried, secretly, in the solitudes of the mountains, in order to conceal the evidences of the deed.

Darius determined on punishing this crime. Some consideration was, however, required, in order to determine in what way his object could best be effected. The province of Oretes was at a great distance from Susa, and

Oretes was strongly established there, at the head of a great force. His guards were bound, it is true, to obey the orders of Darius, but it was questionable whether they would do so. To raise an army and march against the rebellious governor would be an expensive and hazardous undertaking, and perhaps, too, it would prove that such a measure was not necessary. All things considered, Darius determined to try the experiment of acting, by his own direct orders, upon the troops and guards in Oretes's capital, with the intention of resorting subsequently to an armed force of his own, if that should be at last required.

He accordingly called together a number of his officers and nobles, selecting those on whose resolution and fidelity he could most confidently rely, and made the following address to them:

"I have an enterprise which I wish to commit to the charge of some one of your number who is willing to undertake it, which requires no military force, and no violent measures of any kind, but only wisdom, sagacity, and courage. I wish to have Oretes, the governor of Sardis, brought to me, dead or alive. He has perpetrated innumerable crimes, and now, in addition to all his other deeds of treacherous violence, he has had the intolerable insolence to put to death one of my messengers. Which of you will volunteer to bring him, dead or alive, to me?"

This proposal awakened a great enthusiasm among the nobles to whom it was addressed. Nearly thirty of them volunteered their services to execute the order. Darius concluded to decide between these competitors by lot. The lot fell upon a certain man named Bagis, and he immediately began to form his plans and make his arrangements for the expedition.

He caused a number of different orders to be prepared, beginning with directions of little moment, and proceeding to commands of more and more weighty importance, all addressed to the officers of Oretes's army and to his guards. These orders were all drawn up in writing with great formality, and were signed by the name of Darius, and sealed with his seal; they, moreover, named Bagis as the officer selected by the king to superintend the execution of them. Provided with these documents, Bagis proceeded to Sardis, and presented himself at the court of Oretes. He presented his own personal credentials, and with them some of his most insignificant orders. Neither

Oretes nor his guards felt any disposition to disobey them. Bagis, being thus received and recognized as the envoy of the king, continued to present new decrees and edicts, from time to time, as occasions occurred in which he thought the guards would be ready to obey them, until he found the habit, on their part, of looking to him as the representative of the supreme power sufficiently established; for their disposition to obey him was not merely tested, it was strengthened by every new act of obedience. When he found, at length, that his hold upon the guards was sufficiently strong, he produced his two final decrees, one ordering the guards to depose Oretes from his power, and the other to behead him. Both the commands were obeyed.

The events and incidents which have been described in this chapter were of no great importance in themselves, but they illustrate, more forcibly than any general description would do the nature and the operation of the government exercised by Darius throughout the vast empire over which he found himself presiding.

Such personal and individual contests and transactions were not all that occupied his attention. He devoted a great deal of thought and of time to the work of arranging, in a distinct and systematic manner, the division of his dominions into provinces, and to regulating precisely the amount of tribute to be required of each, and the modes of collecting it. He divided his empire into twenty great districts, each of which was governed by a ruler called a satrap. He fixed the amount of tribute which each of these districts was to pay, making it greater or less as the soil and the productions of the country varied in fertility and abundance. In some cases this tribute was to be paid in gold, in others in silver, and in others in peculiar commodities, natural to the country of which they were required. For example, one satrapy, which comprised a country famous for its horses, was obliged to furnish one white horse for every day in the year. This made three hundred and sixty annually, that being the number of days in the Persian year. Such a supply, furnished yearly, enabled the king soon to have a very large troop of white horses; and as the horses were beautifully caparisoned, and the riders magnificently armed, the body of cavalry thus formed was one of the most splendid in the world.

The satrapies were numbered from the west toward the east. The western portion of Asia Minor constituted the first, and the East Indian nations the twelfth and last. The East Indians had to pay their tribute in ingots of gold. Their country produced gold.

As it is now forever too late to separate the facts from the fiction of ancient history, and determine what is to be rejected as false and what received as true, our only resource is to tell the whole story just as it comes down to us, leaving it to each reader to decide for himself what he will believe. In this view of the subject, we will conclude this chapter by relating the manner in which it was said in ancient times that these Indian nations obtained their gold.

The gold country was situated in remote and dreary deserts, inhabited only by wild beasts and vermin, among which last there was, it seems, a species of ants, which were of enormous size, and wonderful fierceness and voracity, and which could run faster than the fleetest horse or camel. These ants, in making their excavations, would bring up from beneath the surface of the ground all the particles of gold which came in their way, and throw them out around their hills. The Indians then would penetrate into these deserts, mounted on the fleetest camels that they could procure, and leading other camels, not so fleet, by their sides. They were provided, also, with bags for containing the golden sands. When they arrived at the ant hills, they would dismount, and, gathering up the gold which the ants had discarded, would fill their bags with the utmost possible dispatch, and then mount their camels and ride away. The ants, in the mean time, would take the alarm, and begin to assemble to attack them; but as their instinct prompted them to wait until considerable numbers were collected before they commenced their attack, the Indians had time to fill their bags and begin their flight before their enemies were ready. Then commenced the chase, the camels running at their full speed, and the swarms of ants following, and gradually drawing nearer and nearer. At length, when nearly overtaken, the Indians would abandon the camels that they were leading, and fly on, more swiftly, upon those which they rode. While the ants were busy in devouring the victims thus given up to them, the authors of all the mischief would make good their escape, and thus carry off their gold to a place of safety. These famous ants were bigger than foxes!

CHAPTER VI.

THE RECONNOITERING OF GREECE.

B.C. 519

The reconnoitering party.--The physician Democedes.--Story of Democedes.--His boyhood.--Democedes at 艾 ina.--At Athens.--At the court of Polycrates.--Democedes a captive.--He is sent to Darius.--Democedes is cast into prison.--His wretched condition.--Darius sprains his ankle.--The Egyptian physicians baffled.--Sufferings of Darius.--He sends for Democedes.--Democedes's denial.--He treats the sprain successfully.--Darius's recovery.--The golden fetters.--Democedes released.--Honors conferred on him.--Atossa cured by Democedes.--His conditions.--Atossa with Darius.--She suggests the invasion of Greece.--The exploring party.--Democedes appointed guide.--Designs of Democedes.--Darius baffled.--The expedition sets out.--City of Sidon.--The sea voyage.--The Grecian coasts examined.--Arrival at Tarentum.--Suspicions of the authorities.--The Persians seized.--Escape of Democedes.--Release of the Persians.--Tumult at Crotona.--Conduct of Democedes.--The expedition returns.--Misfortunes.--Cillus.--Arrival at Susa.--Reception by Darius.

The great event in the history of Darius--the one, in fact, on account of which it was, mainly, that his name and his career have been so widely celebrated among mankind, was an attempt which he made, on a very magnificent scale, for the invasion and conquest of Greece. Before commencing active operations in this grand undertaking, he sent a reconnoitering party to examine and explore the ground. This reconnoitering party met with a variety of extraordinary adventures in the course of its progress, and the history of it will accordingly form the subject of this chapter.

The guide to this celebrated reconnoitering party was a certain Greek physician named Democedes. Though Democedes was called a Greek, he was, really, an Italian by birth. His native town was Crotona, which may be found exactly at the ball of the foot on the map of Italy. It was by a very singular series of adventures that he passed from this remote village in the west, over thousands of miles by land and sea, to Susa, Darius's capital. He began by running away from his father while he was still a boy. He said that he was driven to this step by the intolerable strictness and cruelty of his father's government. This, however, is always the pretext of turbulent and ungovernable young men, who abandon their parents and their homes when the favors and the protection necessary during their long and helpless infancy have been all received, and the time is beginning to arrive for making some return.

Democedes was ingenious and cunning, and fond of roving adventure. In running away from home, he embarked on board a ship, as such characters generally do at the present day, and went to sea. After meeting with various adventures, he established himself in the island of Aina, in the 茨 ean sea, where he began to practice as a physician, though he had had no regular education in that art. In his practice he evinced so much medical skill, or, at least, exercised so much adroitness in leading people to believe that he possessed it, as to give him very soon a wide and exalted reputation. The people of Aina appointed him their physician, and assigned him a large salary for his services in attending upon the sick throughout the island. This was the usual practice in those days. A town, or an island, or any circumscribed district of country, would appoint a physician as a public officer, who was to devote his attention, at a fixed annual salary, to any cases of sickness which might arise in the community, wherever his services were needed, precisely as physicians serve in hospitals and public institutions in modern times.

Democedes remained at Aina two years, during which time his celebrity increased and extended more and more, until, at length, he received an appointment from the city of Athens, with the offer of a greatly increased salary. He accepted the appointment, and remained in Athens one year, when he received still more advantageous offers from Polycrates, the king of Samos, whose history was given so fully in the last chapter.

Democedes remained for some time in the court of Polycrates, where he was raised to the highest distinction, and loaded with many honors. He was a member of the household of the king, enjoyed his confidence in a high degree, and attended him, personally, on all his expeditions. At last, when Polycrates went to Sardis, as is related in the last chapter, to receive the treasures of Oretes, and concert with him the plans for their proposed campaigns, Democedes accompanied him as usual; and when Polycrates was slain, and his attendants and followers were made captive by Oretes, the unfortunate physician was among the number. By this reverse, he found that he had suddenly fallen from affluence, ease, and honor, to the condition of a neglected and wretched captive in the hands of a malignant and merciless tyrant.

Democedes pined in this confinement for a long time; when, at length, Oretes himself was killed by the order of Darius, it might have been expected that the hour of his deliverance had arrived. But it was not so; his condition was, in fact, made worse, and not better by it; for Bag 鴒 s, the commissioner of Darius, instead of inquiring into the circumstances relating to the various members of Oretes's family, and redressing the wrongs which any of them might be suffering, simply seized the whole company, and brought them all to Darius in Susa, as trophies of his triumph, and tokens of the faithfulness and efficiency with which he had executed the work that Darius had committed to his charge. Thus Democedes was borne away, in hopeless bondage, thousands of miles farther from his native land than before, and with very little prospect of being ever able to return. He arrived at Susa, destitute, squalid, and miserable. His language was foreign, his rank and his professional skill unknown, and all the marks which might indicate the refinement and delicacy of the modes of life to which he had been accustomed were wholly disguised by his present destitution and wretchedness. He was sent with the other captives to the prisons, where he was secured, like them, with fetters and chains, and was soon almost entirely forgotten.

He might have taken some measures for making his character, and his past celebrity and fame as a physician known; but he did not dare to do this, for fear that Darius might learn to value his medical skill, and so detain him as a slave for the sake of his services. He thought that the chance was greater that some turn of fortune, or some accidental change in the arrangements of government might take place, by which he might be set at liberty, as an insignificant and worthless captive, whom there was no particular motive for detaining, than if he were transferred to the king's household as a slave, and his value as an artisan--for medical practice was, in those days, simply an art-- were once known. He made no effort, therefore, to bring his true character to light, but pined silently in his dungeon, in rags and wretchedness, and in a mental despondency which was gradually sinking into despair.

About this time, it happened that Darius was one day riding furiously in a chase, and coming upon some sudden danger, he attempted to leap from his horse. He fell and sprained his ankle. He was taken up by the attendants, and carried home. His physicians were immediately called to attend to the case. They were Egyptians. Egypt was, in fact, considered the great seat and centre of learning and of the arts in those days, and no royal household was complete without Egyptian physicians.

The learning and skill, however, of the Egyptians in Darius's court were entirely baffled by the sprain. They thought that the joint was dislocated, and they turned and twisted the foot with so much violence, in their attempts to restore the bones to their proper position, as greatly to increase the pain and the inflammation. Darius spent a week in extreme and excruciating suffering. He could not sleep day nor night, but tossed in continual restlessness and anguish on his couch, made constantly worse instead of better by every effort of his physicians to relieve him.

At length somebody informed him that there was a Greek physician among the captives that came from Sardis, and recommended that Darius should send for him. The king, in his impatience and pain, was ready for any experiment which promised the least hope of relief, and he ordered that Democedes should be immediately summoned. The officers accordingly went to the prison and brought out the astonished captive, without any notice or preparation, and conducted him, just as he was, ragged and wretched, and shackled with iron fetters upon his feet, into the presence of the king. The fetters which such captives wore were intended to allow them to walk, slowly and with difficulty, while they impeded the movements of the feet so as effectually to prevent any long or rapid flight, or any escape at all from free pursuers.

Democedes, when questioned by Darius, denied at first that he possessed any medical knowledge or skill. Darius was, however, not deceived by these protestations. It was very customary, in those days of royal tyranny, for those who possessed any thing valuable to conceal the possession of it: concealment was often their only protection. Darius, who was well aware of this tendency, did not believe the assurances of Democedes, and in the irritation and impatience caused by his pain, he ordered the captive to be taken out and put to the torture, in order to make him confess that he was really a physician.

Democedes yielded without waiting to be actually put to the test. He acknowledged at once, for fear of the torture, that he had had some experience in medical practice, and the sprained ankle was immediately committed to his charge. On examining the case, he thought that the harsh and violent operations which the Egyptian physicians had attempted were not required. He treated the inflamed and swollen joint in the gentlest manner. He made fomenting and emollient applications, which soothed the pain, subdued the inflammation, and allayed the restlessness and the fever. The royal sufferer became quiet and calm, and in a short time fell asleep.

In a word, the king rapidly recovered; and, overwhelmed with gratitude toward the benefactor whose skill had saved him from such suffering, he ordered that, in place of his single pair of iron fetters, he should have two pairs of fetters of gold!

It might at first be imagined that such a strange token of regard as this could be intended only as a jest and an insult; but there is no doubt that Darius meant it seriously as a compliment and an honor. He supposed that Democedes, of course, considered his condition of captivity as a fixed and permanent one; and that his fetters were not, in themselves, an injustice or disgrace, but the necessary and unavoidable concomitant of his lot, so that the sending of golden fetters to a slave was very naturally, in his view, like presenting a golden crutch to a cripple. Democedes received the equivocal donation with great good nature. He even ventured upon a joke on the subject to the convalescent king. "It seems, sire," said he "that in return for my saving your limb and your life, you double my servitude. You have given me two chains instead of one."

The king, who was now in a much better humor to be pleased than when, writhing in anguish, he had ordered Democedes to be put to the torture, laughed at this reply, and released the captive from the bonds entirely. He ordered him to be conducted by the attendants to the apartments of the palace, where the wives of Darius and the other ladies of the court resided, that they might see him and express their gratitude. "This is the physician," said the eunuchs, who introduced him, "that cured the king." The ladies welcomed him with the utmost cordiality, and loaded him with presents of gold and silver as he passed through their apartments. The king made arrangements, too, immediately, for providing him with a magnificent house in Susa, and established him there in great luxury and splendor, with costly furniture and many attendants, and all other marks of distinction and honor. In a word, Democedes found himself, by means of another unexpected change of fortune, suddenly elevated to a height as lofty as his misery and degradation had been low. He was, however, a captive still.

The Queen Atossa, the daughter of Cyrus, who has already been mentioned as the wife of Cambyses and of Smerdis the magian, was one of the wives of Darius. Her sister Antystone was another. A third was Ph鎬yma, the daughter of Otanes, the lady who had been so instrumental, in connection with Atossa, in the discovery of the magian imposture. It happened that, some time after the curing of Darius's sprain, Atossa herself was sick. Her malady was of such a nature, that for some time she kept it concealed, from a feeling of delicacy.[E] At length, terrified by the danger which threatened her, she sent for Democedes, and made her case known to him. He said that he could cure her, but she must first promise to grant him, if he did so, a certain favor which he should ask. She must promise beforehand to grant it, whatever it might be. It was nothing, he said, that should in any way compromise her honor.

[Footnote E: It was a tumor of the breast, which became, at length, an open ulcer, and began to spread and enlarge in a very formidable manner.]

Atossa agreed to these conditions, and Democedes undertook her case. Her malady was soon cured; and when she asked him what was the favor which he wished to demand, he replied,

"Persuade Darius to form a plan for the invasion of Greece, and to send me, with a small company of attendants, to explore the country, and obtain for him all the necessary preliminary information. In this way I shall see my native land once more."

Atossa was faithful in her promise. She availed herself of the first favorable opportunity, when it became her turn to visit the king, to direct his mind, by a dexterous conversation, toward the subject of the enlargement of his empire. He had vast forces and resources, she said, at his command, and might easily enter upon a career of conquest which would attract the admiration of the world. Darius replied that he had been entertaining some views of that nature. He had thought, he said, of attacking the Scythians: these Scythians were a group of semi-savage nations on the north of his dominions. Atossa represented to him that subduing the Scythians would be too easy a conquest, and that it would be a far nobler enterprise, and more worthy of his talents and his vast resources, to undertake an expedition into Europe, and attempt the conquest of Greece. "You have all the means at your command essential for the success of such an undertaking, and you have in your court a man who can give you, or can obtain for you, all the necessary information in respect to the country, to enable you to form the plan of your campaigns."

The ambition of Darius was fired by these suggestions. He began immediately to form projects and schemes. In a day or two he organized a small party of Persian officers of distinction, in whom he had great confidence, to go on an exploring tour into Greece. They were provided with a suitable company of attendants, and with every thing necessary for their journey, and Democedes was directed to prepare to go with them as their guide. They were to travel simply as a party of Persian noblemen, on an excursion of curiosity and pleasure, concealing their true design; and as Democedes their guide, though born in Italy, was in all important points a Greek, and was well acquainted with the countries through which they were to pass, they supposed that they could travel every where without suspicion. Darius charged the Persians to keep a diligent watch over Democedes, and not to allow him, on any account to leave them, but to bring him back to Susa safely with them on their return.

As for Democedes, he had no intention whatever of returning to Persia, though he kept his designs of making his escape entirely concealed. Darius, with seeming generosity, said to him, while he was making his preparations, "I recommend to you to take with you all your private wealth and treasures, to distribute, for presents, among your friends in Greece and Italy. I will bestow more upon you here on your return." Democedes regarded this counsel with great suspicion. He imagined that the king, in giving him this permission, wished to ascertain, by observing whether he would really take with him all his possessions, the existence of any secret determination in his mind not to come back to Susa. If this were Darius's plan, it was defeated by the sagacious vigilance and cunning of the physician. He told the king, in reply, that he preferred to leave his effects in Persia, that they might be ready for his use on his return. The king then ordered a variety of costly articles to be provided and given to Democedes, to be taken with him and presented to his friends in Greece and Italy. They consisted of vessels of gold and silver, pieces of Persian armor of beautiful workmanship, and articles of dress, expensive and splendid. These were all carefully packed, and the various other necessary preparations were made for the long journey.

At length the expedition set out. They traveled by land westward, across the continent, till they reached the eastern shores of the Mediterranean Sea. The port at which they arrived was Sidon, the city so often mentioned in the Scriptures as a great pagan emporium of commerce. The city of Sidon was in the height of its glory at this time, being one of the most important ports of the Mediterranean for all the western part of Asia. Caravans of travelers came to it by land, bringing on the backs of camels the productions of Arabia, Persia, and all the East; and fleets of ships by sea, loaded with the corn, and wine, and oil of the Western nations.

At Sidon the land journey of the expedition was ended. Here they bought two large and splendid ships, galleys of three banks of oars, to convey them to Greece. These galleys were for their own personal accommodation. There was a third vessel, called a transport, for the conveyance of their baggage, which consisted mainly of the packages of rich and costly presents which Darius had prepared. Some of these presents were for the friends of Democedes, as has been already explained, and others had been provided as gifts and offerings from the king himself to such distinguished personages as the travelers might visit on their route. When the vessels were ready, and the costly cargo was on board, the company of travelers embarked, and the little fleet put to sea.

The Grecian territories are endlessly divided and indented by the seas, whose irregular and winding shores form promontories, peninsulas, and islands without number, which are accessible in every part by water. The Persian explorers cruised about among these coasts under Democedes's guidance, examining every thing, and noting carefully all the information which they could obtain, either by personal observation or by inquiring of others, which might be of service to Darius in his intended invasion. Democedes allowed them to take their own time, directing their course, however, steadily, though slowly, toward his own native town of Crotona. The expedition landed in various places, and were every where well received.

It was not for the interest of Democedes that they should yet be intercepted. In fact, the name and power of Darius were very much feared, or, at least, very highly respected in all the Grecian territory, and the people were little inclined to molest a peaceful party of Persians traveling like ordinary tourists, and under the guidance, too, of a distinguished countryman of their own, whose name was, in some degree, a guarantee for the honesty and innocence of their intentions. At length, however, after spending some time in the Grecian seas, the little squadron moved still farther west, toward the coast of Italy, and arrived finally at Tarentum. Tarentum was the great port on the Grecian side of Italy. It was at the head of the spacious bay which sets up between the heel and the ball of the foot of the boot-shaped peninsula. Crotona, Democedes's native town, to which he was now desirous to return, was southwest of Tarentum, about two hundred miles along the shore.[F]

[Footnote F: For the situation of these places, see the map at the commencement of chapter xi.]

It was a very curious and extraordinary circumstance that, though the expedition had been thus far allowed to go and come as its leaders pleased, without any hinderance or suspicion, yet now, the moment that they touched a point from which Democedes could easily reach his home, the authorities on shore, in some way or other, obtained some intimation of the true character of their enterprise. The Prince of Tarentum seized the ships. He made the Persians themselves prisoners also, and shut them up; and, in order effectually to confine the ships, he took away the helms from them, so that they could not be steered, and were thus entirely disabled. The expedition being thus, for the time at least, broken up, Democedes said, coolly, that he would take the opportunity to make a little excursion along the coast, and visit his friends at Crotona!

It was another equally suspicious circumstance in respect to the probability that this seizure was the result of Democedes's management, that, as soon as he was safely away, the Prince of Tarentum set his prisoners at liberty, releasing, at the same time, the ships from the seizure, and sending the helms on board. The Persians were indignant at the treatment which they had received, and set sail immediately along the coast toward Crotona in pursuit of Democedes. They found him in the market-place in Crotona, haranguing the people, and exciting, by his appearance and his discourse, a great and general curiosity. They attempted to seize him as a fugitive, and called upon the people of Crotona to aid them, threatening them with the vengeance of Darius if they refused. A part of the people were disposed to comply with this demand, while others rallied to defend their townsman. A great tumult ensued; but, in the end, the party of Democedes was victorious. He was not only thus personally rescued, but, as he informed the people that the transport vessel which accompanied the expedition contained property that belonged to him, they seized that too, and gave it up to Democedes, saying to the Persians that, though they must give up the transport, the galleys remained at their service to convey them back to their own country whenever they wished to go.

The Persians had now no other alternative but to return home. They had, it is true, pretty nearly accomplished the object of their undertaking; but, if any thing remained to be done, they could not now attempt it with any advantage, as they had lost their guide, and a great portion of the effects which had been provided by Darius to enable them to propitiate the favor of the princes and potentates into whose power they might fall. They accordingly began to make preparations for sailing back again to Sidon, while Democedes established himself in great magnificence and splendor in Crotona. When, at length, the Persians were ready to sail, Democedes wished them a very pleasant voyage, and desired them to give his best respects to Darius, and inform him that he could not return at present to Persia, as he was making arrangements to be married!

The disasters which had befallen these Persian reconnoiterers thus far were only the beginning of their troubles. Their ships were driven by contrary winds out of their course, and they were thrown at last upon the coast of Iapygia, a country occupying the heel of Italy. Here they were seized by the inhabitants and made slaves. It happened that there was living in this wild country at that time a man of wealth and of cultivation, who had been exiled from Tarentum on account of some political offenses. His name was Cillus. He heard the story of these unhappy foreigners, and interested himself in their fate. He thought that, by rescuing them from their captivity and sending them home, he should make Darius his friend, and secure, perhaps, his aid in effecting his own restoration to his native land. He accordingly paid the ransom which was demanded for the captives, and set them free. He then aided them in making arrangements for their return to Persia, and the unfortunate messengers found their way back at last to the court of Darius, without their guide, without any of the splendid appointments with which they had gone forth, but stripped of every thing, and glad to escape with their lives.

They had some cause to fear, too, the anger of Darius, for the insensate wrath of a tyrant is awakened as often by calamity as by crime. Darius, however, was in this instance graciously disposed. He received the unfortunate commissioners in a favorable manner. He took immediate measures for rewarding Cillus for having ransomed them. He treasured up, too, the information which they had obtained respecting Greece, though he was prevented by circumstances, which we will proceed to describe, from immediately putting into execution his plans of invasion and conquest there.

CHAPTER VII.

THE REVOLT OF BABYLON.

B.C. 516-514

City of Babylon.--The captive Jews.--Wickedness of the Babylonians.--Causes of discontent.--Preparations of the Babylonians for revolt.--Their secrecy.--Time chosen for revolt.--Story of Syloson.--Syloson's red cloak.--He gives it to Darius.--Syloson goes to Susa.--Interview with Darius.--Request of Syloson.--Darius grants it.--Citadel of Samos.--Measures of Mendrius.--Hypocrisy of Mendrius.--His brother Charilaus.--Reproaches of Charilaus.--Character of Mendrius.--Attack of Charilaus.--Slaughter of the Samians.--Revolt of Babylon.--Insults and jeers of the Babylonians.--Ancient mode of warfare.--Modern warfare.--Taunt of the Babylonians.--Fabricating prodigies.--The mule of Zopyrus.--Interview with Darius.--Desperate plan of Zopyrus.--He mutilates himself.--Darius's astonishment.--Final arrangements.--Zopyrus leaves the Persian camp.--Success of Zopyrus's stratagem.--His piteous story.--The three victories.--Zopyrus intrusted with power in Babylon.--Zopyrus admits the Persians.--Fall of Babylon.

The city of Babylon, originally the capital of the Assyrian empire, was conquered by Cyrus, the founder of the Persian monarchy, when he annexed the Assyrian empire to his dominions. It was a vast and a very magnificent and wealthy city; and Cyrus made it, for a time, one of his capitals.

When Cyrus made this conquest of Babylon, he found the Jews in captivity there. They had been made captive by Nebuchadnezzar, a previous king of Babylon, as is related in the Scriptures. The holy prophets of Judea had predicted that after seventy years the captives should return, and that Babylon itself should afterward be destroyed. The first prediction was fulfilled by the victory of Cyrus. It devolved on Darius to execute the second of these solemn and retributive decrees of heaven.

Although Darius was thus the instrument of divine Providence in the destruction of Babylon, he was unintentionally and unconsciously so. In the terrible scenes connected with the siege and the storming of the ill-fated city, it was the impulse of his own hatred and revenge that he was directly obeying; he was not at all aware that he was, at the same time, the messenger of the divine displeasure. The wretched Babylonians, in the storming and destruction of their city, were expiating a double criminality. Their pride, their wickedness, their wanton cruelty toward the Jews, had brought upon them the condemnation of God, while their political treason and rebellion, or, at least, what was considered treason and rebellion aroused the implacable resentment of their king.

The Babylonians had been disposed to revolt even in the days of Cyrus. They had been accustomed to consider their city as the most noble and magnificent capital in the world, and they were displeased that Cyrus did not make it the seat and center of his empire. Cyrus preferred Susa; and Babylon, accordingly, though he called it one of his capitals, soon fell to the rank of a provincial city. The nobles and provincial leaders that remained there began accordingly to form plans for revolting from the Persian dominion, with a view of restoring their city to its ancient position and renown.

They had a very favorable opportunity for maturing their plans, and making their preparations for the execution of them during the time of the magian usurpation; for while the false Smerdis was on the throne, being shut up and concealed in his palace at Susa, the affairs of the provinces were neglected; and when Darius and his accomplices discovered the imposture and put Smerdis to death, there was necessarily required, after so violent a revolution, a considerable time before the affairs of the empire demanding attention at the capital could be settled, so as to allow the government to turn their thoughts at all toward the distant dependencies. The Babylonians availed themselves of all these opportunities to put their city in the best condition for resisting the Persian power. They strengthened their defenses, and accumulated great stores of provisions, and took measures for diminishing that part of the population which would be useless in war. These measures were all concerted and carried into effect in the most covert and secret manner; and the tidings came at last to Susa that Babylon had openly revolted, before the government of Darius was aware even of the existence of any disaffection.

The time which the Babylonians chose for their rebellion at last was one when the movable forces which Darius had at command were at the west, engaged in a campaign on the shores of Asia Minor. Darius had sent them there for the purpose of restoring a certain exile and wanderer named Syloson to Samos, and making him the monarch of it. Darius had been induced thus to interpose in Syloson's behalf by the following very extraordinary circumstances.

Syloson was the brother of Polycrates, whose unhappy history has already been given. He was exiled from Samos some time before Darius ascended the throne, and he became, consequently, a sort of soldier of fortune, serving, like other such adventurers, wherever there was the greatest prospect of glory and pay. In this capacity he followed the army of Cambyses into Egypt in the memorable campaign described in the first chapter of this volume. It happened, also, that Darius himself, who was then a young noble in the Persian court, and yet of no particular distinction, as there was then no reason to imagine that he would ever be elevated to the throne, was also in Cambyses's army, and the two young men became acquainted with one another there.

While the army was at Memphis, an incident occurred in which these two personages were actors, which, though it seemed unimportant at the time, led, in the end, to vast and momentous results. The incident was this:

Syloson had a very handsome red cloak, which, as he appeared in it one day, walking in the great square at Memphis, strongly attracted the admiration of Darius. Darius asked Syloson if he would sell him the cloak. Syloson said that he would not sell it, but would give it to him. He thought, probably, that Darius would decline receiving it as a present. If he did entertain that idea, it seems he was mistaken. Darius praised him for his generosity, and accepted the gift.

Syloson was then sorry that he had made so inconsiderate an offer, and regretted very much the loss of his cloak. In process of time, the campaign of Cambyses in Egypt was ended, and Darius returned to Persia, leaving Syloson in the west. At length the conspiracy was formed for dethroning Smerdis the magian, as has already been described, and Darius was designated to reign in his stead. As the news of the young noble's elevation spread into the western world, it reached Syloson. He was much pleased at receiving the intelligence, and he saw immediately that there was a prospect of his being able to derive some advantage, himself, from the accession of his old fellow-soldier to the throne.

He immediately proceeded to Susa. He applied at the gates of the palace for admission to the presence of the king. The porter asked him who he was. He replied that he was a Greek who had formerly done Darius a service, and he wished to see him. The porter carried the message to the king. The king could not imagine who the stranger should be. He endeavored in vain to recall to mind any instance in which he had received a favor from a Greek. At length he ordered the attendant to call the visitor in.

Syloson was accordingly conducted into the king's presence. Darius looked upon him, but did not know him. He directed the interpreters to inquire what the service was which he had rendered the king, and when he had rendered it. The Greek replied by relating the circumstance of the cloak. Darius recollected the cloak, though he had forgotten the giver. "Are you, indeed," said he, "the man who made me that present? I thought then that you were very generous to me, and you shall see that I do not undervalue the obligation now. I am at length, fortunately, in a situation to requite the favor, and I will give you such an abundance of gold and silver as shall effectually prevent your being sorry for having shown a kindness to Darius Hystaspes."

Syloson thanked the king in reply, but said that he did not wish for gold and silver. Darius asked him what reward he did desire. He replied that he wished Samos to be restored to him: "Samos," said he, "was the possession of my brother. When he went away from the island, he left it temporarily in the hands of Mendrius, an officer of his household. It still remains in the possession of this family, while I, the rightful heir, am a homeless wanderer and exile, excluded from my brother's dominions by one of his slaves."

Darius immediately determined to accede to Syloson's request. He raised an army and put it under the command of Otanes, who, it will be recollected, was one of the seven conspirators that combined to dethrone Smerdis the magian. He directed Otanes to accompany Syloson to Samos, and to put him in possession of the island. Syloson was particularly earnest in his request that no unnecessary violence should be used, and no blood shed, or vindictive measures of any kind adopted. Darius promised to comply with these desires, and gave his orders to Otanes accordingly.

Notwithstanding this, however, the expedition resulted in the almost total destruction of the Samian population, in the following manner. There was a citadel at Samos, to which the inhabitants retired when they learned that Otanes had embarked his troops in ships on the coast, and was advancing toward the island. Mendrius was vexed and angry at the prospect of being deprived of his possessions and his power; and, as the people hated him on account of his extortion and tyranny, he hated them in return, and cared not how much suffering his measures might be the means of bringing upon them. He had a subterranean and secret passage from the citadel to the shore of the sea, where, in a secluded cove, were boats or vessels ready to take him away. Having made these arrangements to secure his own safety, he proceeded to take such a course and adopt such measures as should tend most effectually to exasperate and offend the Persians, intending to escape, himself, at the last moment, by this subterranean retreat, and to leave the inhabitants of the island at the mercy of their infuriated enemies.

He had a brother whom he had shut up in a dungeon, and whose mind, naturally depraved, and irritated by his injuries, was in a state of malignant and furious despair. Mendrius had pretended to be willing to give up the island to the Persians. He had entered into negotiations with them for this purpose, and the Persians considered the treaty as in fact concluded. The leaders and officers of the army had assembled, accordingly, before the citadel in a peaceful attitude, waiting merely for the completion of the forms of surrender, when Charilaus, Mendrius's captive brother, saw them, by looking out between the bars of his window, in the tower in which he was confined. He sent an urgent message to Mendrius, requesting to speak to him. Mendrius ordered the prisoner to be brought before him. The haggard and wretched-looking captive, rendered half insane by the combined influence of the confinement he had endured, and of the wild excitement produced by the universal panic and confusion which reigned around him, broke forth against his brother in the boldest and most violent invectives. He reproached him in the most bitter terms for being willing to yield so ingloriously, and without a struggle, to an invading foe, whom he might easily repel. "You have courage and energy enough, it seems," said he, "to make war upon an innocent and defenseless brother, and to keep him for years in chains and in a dungeon, but when an actual enemy appears, though he comes to despoil you of all your possessions, and to send you into hopeless exile, and though, if you had the ordinary courage and spirit of a man, you could easily drive him away, yet you dare not face him. If you are too cowardly and mean to do your duty yourself, give me your soldiers, and I will do it for you. I will drive these Persians back into the sea with as much pleasure as it would give me to drive you there!"

Such a nature as that of Mendrius can not be stung into a proper sense of duty by reproaches like these. There seem to have been in his heart no moral sensibilities of any kind, and there could be, of course, no compunctions for the past, and no awakening of new and better desires for the future. All the effect which was produced upon his mind by these bitter denunciations was to convince him that to comply with his brother's request would be to do the best thing now in his power for widening, and extending, and making sure the misery and mischief which were impending. He placed his troops, therefore, under his brother's orders; and while the infuriated madman sallied forth at the head of them to attack the astonished Persians on one side of the citadel, Mendrius made his escape through the under-ground passage on the other. The Persians were so exasperated at what appeared to them the basest treachery, that, as soon as they could recover their arms and get once more into battle array, they commenced a universal slaughter of the Samians. They spared neither age, sex, nor condition; and when, at last, their vengeance was satisfied, and they put the island into Syloson's hands, and withdrew, he found himself in possession of an almost absolute solitude.

It was while Otanes was absent on this enterprise, having with him a large part of the disposable forces of the king, that the Babylonians revolted. Darius was greatly incensed at hearing the tidings. Sovereigns are always greatly incensed at a revolt on the part of their subjects. The circumstances of the case, whatever they may be, always seem to them to constitute a peculiar aggravation of the offense. Darius was indignant that the Babylonians had attempted to take advantage of his weakness by rebelling when his armies were away. If they had risen when his armies were around him, he would have been equally indignant with them for having dared to brave his power.

He assembled all the forces at his disposal, and advanced to Babylon. The people of the city shut their gates against him, and derided him. They danced and capered on the walls, making all sorts of gestures expressive of contempt and defiance, accompanied with shouts and outcries of ridicule and scorn. They had great confidence in the strength of their defenses, and then, besides this, they probably regarded Darius as a sort of usurper, who had no legitimate title to the throne, and who would never be able to subdue any serious resistance which might be offered to the establishment of his power. It was from these considerations that they were emboldened to be guilty of the folly of taunting and insulting their foes from the city walls.

Such incidents as this, of personal communications between masses of enemies on the eve of a battle, were very common in ancient warfare, though impossible in modern times. In those days, when the missiles employed were thrown chiefly by the strength of the human arm alone, the combatants could safely draw near enough together for each side to hear the voices and to see the gesticulations of the other. Besiegers could advance sufficiently close to a castle or citadel to parley insultingly with the garrison upon the walls, and yet be safe from the showers of darts and arrows which were projected toward them in return. But all this is now changed. The reach of cannon, and even of musketry, is so long, that combatants, approaching a conflict, are kept at a very respectful distance apart, until the time arrives in which the actual engagement is to begin. They reconnoiter each other with spy-glasses from watch-towers on the walls, or from eminences in the field, but they can hold no communication except by a formal embassy, protected by a flag of truce, which, with its white and distant fluttering, as it slowly advances over the green fields, warns the gunners at the battery or on the bastion to point their artillery another way.

The Babylonians, on the walls of their city, reproached and taunted their foes incessantly. "Take our advice," said they, "and go back where you came from. You will only lose your time in besieging Babylon. When mules have foals, you will take the city, and not till then."

The expression "when mules have foals" was equivalent in those days to our proverbial phrase, "when the sky falls," being used to denote any thing impossible or absurd, inasmuch as mules, like other hybrid animals, do not produce young. It was thought in those times absolutely impossible that they should do so; but it is now well known that the case is not impossible, though very rare.

It seems to have added very much to the interest of an historical narrative in the minds of the ancient Greeks, to have some prodigy connected with every great event; and, in order to gratify this feeling, the writers appear in some instances to have fabricated a prodigy for the occasion, and in others to have elevated some unusual, though by no means supernatural circumstance, to the rank and importance of one. The prodigy connected with this siege of Babylon was the foaling of a mule. The mule belonged to a general in the army of Darius, named Zopyrus. It was after Darius had been prosecuting the siege of the city for a year and a half, without any progress whatever toward the accomplishment of his end. The army began to despair of success. Zopyrus, with the rest, was expecting that the siege would be indefinitely prolonged, or, perhaps, absolutely abandoned, when his attention was strongly attracted to the phenomenon which had happened in respect to the mule. He remembered the taunt of the Babylonian on the wall, and it seemed to him that the whole occurrence portended that the time had now arrived when some way might be devised for the capture of the city.

Portents and prophecies are often the causes of their own fulfillment, and this portent led Zopyrus to endeavor to devise some means to accomplish the end in view. He went first, however, to Darius, to converse with him upon the subject, with a view of ascertaining how far he was really desirous of bringing the siege to a termination. He wished to know whether the object was of sufficient importance in Darius's mind to warrant any great sacrifice on his own part to effect it.

He found that it was so. Darius was extremely impatient to end the siege and to capture the city; and Zopyrus saw at once that, if he could in any way be the means of accomplishing the work, he should entitle himself, in the highest possible degree, to the gratitude of the king.

He determined to go himself into Babylon as a pretended deserter from Darius, with a view to obtaining an influence and a command within the city, which should enable him afterward to deliver it up to the besiegers; and, in order to convince the Babylonians that his desertion was real, he resolved to mutilate himself in a manner so dreadful as would effectually prevent their imagining that the injuries which he suffered were inflicted by any contrivance of his own. He accordingly cut off his hair and his ears, and mutilated his face in a manner too shocking to be here detailed, inflicting injuries which could never be repaired. He caused himself to be scourged, also, until his whole body was covered with cuts and contusions. He then went, wounded and bleeding as he was, into the presence of Darius, to make known his plans.

Darius expressed amazement and consternation at the terrible spectacle. He leaped from his throne and rushed toward Zopyrus, demanding who had dared to maltreat one of his generals in such a manner. When Zopyrus replied that he had himself done the deed, the king's astonishment was greater than before. He told Zopyrus that he was insane. Some sudden paroxysm of madness had come over him. Zopyrus replied that he was not insane; and he explained his design. His plan, he said, was deliberately and calmly formed, and it should be steadily and faithfully executed. "I did not make known my design to you," said he, "before I had taken the preliminary steps, for I knew that you would prevent my taking them. It is now too late for that, and nothing remains but to reap, if possible, the advantage which may be derived from what I have done."

He then arranged with Darius the plans which he had formed, so far as he needed the co-operation of the king in the execution of them. If he could gain a partial command in the Babylonian army, he was to make a sally from the city gates on a certain day, and attack a portion of the Persian army, which Darius was to leave purposely exposed, in order that he might gain credit with the Babylonians by destroying them. From this he supposed that the confidence which the Babylonians would repose in him would increase, and he might consequently receive a greater command. Thus he might, by acting in concert with Darius without, gradually gain such an ascendency within the city as finally to have power to open the gates and let the besiegers in. Darius was to station a detachment of a thousand men near a certain gate, leaving them imperfectly armed, on the tenth day after Zopyrus entered the city. These Zopyrus was to destroy. Seven days afterward, two thousand more were to be stationed in a similar manner at another point; and these were also to be destroyed by a second sally. Twenty days after this, four thousand more were to be similarly exposed. Thus seven thousand innocent and defenseless men would be slaughtered, but that, as Zopyrus said, would be "of no consequence." The lives of men were estimated by heroes and conquerors in those days only at their numerical value in swelling the army roll.

These things being all arranged, Zopyrus took leave of the King to go to Babylon. As he left the Persian camp, he began to run, looking round behind him continually, as if in flight. Some men, too, pretended to pursue him. He fled toward one of the gates of the city. The sentinels on the walls saw him coming. When he reached the gate, the porter inside of it talked with him through a small opening, and heard his story. The porter then reported the case to the superior officers, and they commanded that the fugitive should be admitted. When conducted into the presence of the magistrates, he related a piteous story of the cruel treatment which he had received from Darius, and of the difficulty which he had experienced in making his escape from the tyrant's hands. He uttered, too, dreadful imprecations against Darius, and expressed the most eager determination to be revenged. He informed the Babylonians, moreover, that he was well acquainted with all Darius's plans and designs, and with the disposition which he had made of his army; and that, if they would, in a few days, when his wounds should have in some measure healed, give him a small command, he would show them, by actual trial, what he could do to aid their cause.

They acceded to this proposition, and furnished Zopyrus, at the end of ten days, with a moderate force. Zopyrus, at the head of this force, sallied forth from the gate which had been previously agreed upon between him and Darius, and fell upon the unfortunate thousand that had been stationed there for the purpose of being destroyed. They were nearly defenseless, and Zopyrus, though his force was inferior, cut them all to pieces before they could be re-enforced or protected, and then retreated safely into the city again. He was received by the Babylonians with the utmost exultation and joy. He had no difficulty in obtaining, seven days afterward, the command of a larger force, when, sallying forth from another gate, as had been agreed upon by Darius, he gained another victory, destroying, on this occasion, twice as many Persians as before. These exploits gained the pretended deserter unbounded fame and honor within the city. The populace applauded him with continual acclamations; and the magistrates invited him to their councils, offered him high command, and governed their own plans and measures by his advice. At length, on the twentieth day, he made his third sally, at which time he destroyed and captured a still greater number than before. This gave him such an influence and position within the city, in respect to its defense, that he had no difficulty in getting intrusted with the keys of certain gates-- those, namely, by which he had agreed that the army of Darius should be admitted.

When the time arrived, the Persians advanced to the attack of the city in that quarter, and the Babylonians rallied as usual on the walls to repel them. The contest had scarcely begun before they found that the gates were open, and that the columns of the enemy were pouring in. The city was thus soon wholly at the mercy of the conqueror. Darius dismantled the walls, carried off the brazen gates, and crucified three thousand of the most distinguished inhabitants; then establishing over the rest a government of his own, he withdrew his troops and returned to Susa. He bestowed upon Zopyrus, at Susa, all possible rewards and honors. The marks of his wounds and mutilations could never be effaced, but Darius often said that he would gladly give up twenty Babylons to be able to efface them.

CHAPTER VIII.

THE INVASION OF SCYTHIA.

B.C. 513

Darius's authority fully established throughout his dominions.--The Scythians.--Ancient account of them.--Pictures of savage life.--Their diversity.--Social instincts of man.--Their universality.--Moral sentiments of mankind.--Religious depravity.--Advice of Artabanus.--Emissaries sent forward.--The petition of Oebazus.--Darius's wanton cruelty.--Place of rendezvous.--The fleet of galleys.--Darius's march through Asia Minor.--Monuments.--Arrival at the Bosporus.--The bridge of boats.--Reward of Mandrocles.--The group of statuary.--The Cyanean Islands.--Darius makes an excursion to them.--The two monuments.--Inscriptions on them.--The troops cross the bridge.--Movements of the fleet.--The River Tearus.--Its wonderful sources.--The cairn.--Primitive mode of census-taking.--Instinctive feeling of dependence on a supernatural power.--Strange religious observance.--Arrival at the Danube.--Orders to destroy the bridge.--Counsel of the Grecian general.--The bridge is preserved.--Guard left to protect it.--Singular mode of reckoning.--Probable reason for employing it.--Darius's determination to return before the knots should be all untied.

In the reigns of ancient monarchs and conquerors, it often happened that the first great transaction which called forth their energies was the suppression of a rebellion within their dominions, and the second, an expedition against some ferocious and half-savage nations beyond their frontiers. Darius followed this general example. The suppression of the Babylonian revolt established his authority throughout the whole interior of his empire. If that vast, and populous, and wealthy city was found unable to resist his power, no other smaller province or capital could hope to succeed in the attempt. The whole empire of Asia, therefore, from the capital at Susa, out to the extreme limits and bounds to which Cyrus had extended it, yielded without any further opposition to his sway. He felt strong in his position, and being young and ardent in temperament, he experienced a desire to exercise his strength. For some reason or other, he seems to have been not quite prepared yet to grapple with the Greeks, and he concluded, accordingly, first to test his powers in respect to foreign invasion by a war upon the Scythians. This was an undertaking which required some courage and resolution; for it was while making an incursion into the country of the Scythians that Cyrus, his renowned predecessor, and the founder of the Persian empire, had fallen.

The term Scythians seems to have been a generic designation, applied indiscriminately to vast hordes of half-savage tribes occupying those wild and inhospitable regions of the north, that extended along the shores of the Black and Caspian Seas, and the banks of the Danube. The accounts which are given by the ancient historians of the manners and customs of these people, are very inconsistent and contradictory; as, in fact, the accounts of the characters of savages, and of the habits and usages of savage life, have always been in every age. It is very little that any one cultivated observer can really know, in respect to the phases of character, the thoughts and feelings, the sentiments, the principles and the faith, and even the modes of life, that prevail among uncivilized aborigines living in forests, or roaming wildly over uninclosed and trackless plains. Of those who have the opportunity to observe them, accordingly, some extol, in the highest degree, their rude but charming simplicity, their truth and faithfulness, the strength of their filial and conjugal affection, and their superiority of spirit in rising above the sordid sentiments and gross vices of civilization. They are not the slaves, these writers say, of appetite and passion. They have no inordinate love of gain; they are patient in enduring suffering, grateful for kindness received, and inflexibly firm in their adherence to the principles of honor and duty. Others, on the other hand, see in savage life nothing but treachery, cruelty, brutality, and crime. Man in his native state, as they imagine, is but a beast, with just intelligence enough to give effect to his depravity. Without natural affection, without truth, without a sense of justice, or the means of making law a substitute for it, he lives in a scene of continual conflict, in which the rights of the weak and the defenseless are always overborne by brutal and tyrannical power.

The explanation of this diversity is doubtless this, that in savage life, as well as in every other state of human society, all the varieties of human conduct and character are exhibited; and the attention of each observer is attracted to the one or to the other class of phenomena, according to the circumstances in which he is placed when he makes his observations, or the mood of mind which prevails within him when he records them. There must be the usual virtues of social life, existing in a greater or less degree, in all human communities; for such principles as a knowledge of the distinction of right and wrong, the idea of property and of individual rights, the obligation resting on every one to respect them, the sense of justice, and of the ill desert of violence and cruelty, are all universal instincts of the human soul, as universal and as essential to humanity as maternal or filial affection, or the principle of conjugal love. They were established by the great Author of nature as constituent elements in the formation of man. Man could not continue to exist, as a gregarious animal, without them. It would accordingly be as impossible to find a community of men without these moral sentiments generally prevalent among them, as to find vultures or tigers that did not like to pursue and take their prey, or deer without a propensity to fly from danger. The laws and usages of civilized society are the expression and the result of these sentiments, not the origin and foundation of them; and violence, cruelty, and crime are the exceptions to their operation, very few, in all communities, savage or civilized, in comparison with the vast preponderance of cases in which they are obeyed.

This view of the native constitution of the human character, which it is obvious, on very slight reflection, must be true, is not at all opposed, as it might at first appear to be, by the doctrine of the theological writers in the Christian Church in respect to the native depravity of man; for the depravity here referred to is a religious depravity, an alienation of the heart from God, and a rebellious and insubmissive spirit in respect to his law. Neither the Scriptures nor the theological writers who interpret them ever call in question the universal existence and prevalence of those instincts that are essential to the social welfare of man.

But we must return to the Scythians.

The tribes which Darius proposed to attack occupied the countries north of the Danube. His route, therefore, for the invasion of their territories would lead him through Asia Minor, thence across the Hellespont or the Bosporus into Thrace, and from Thrace across the Danube. It was a distant and dangerous expedition.

Darius had a brother named Artabanus. Artabanus was of opinion that the enterprise which the king was contemplating was not only distant and dangerous, but that the country of the Scythians was of so little value that the end to be obtained by success would be wholly inadequate to compensate for the exertions, the costs, and the hazards which he must necessarily incur in the prosecution of it. But Darius was not to be dissuaded. He thanked his brother for his advice, but ordered the preparations for the expedition to go on.

He sent emissaries forward, in advance, over the route that his army was destined to take, transmitting orders to the several provinces which were situated on the line of his march to prepare the way for the passage of his troops. Among other preparations, they were to construct a bridge of boats across the Bosporus at Chalcedon. This work was intrusted to the charge and superintendence of an engineer of Samos named Mandrocles. The people of the provinces were also to furnish bodies of troops, both infantry and cavalry, to join the army on its march.

The soldiers that were enlisted to go on this remote and dangerous expedition joined the army, as is usual in such cases, some willingly, from love of adventure, or the hope of opportunities for plunder, and for that unbridled indulgence of appetite and passion which soldiers so often look forward to as a part of their reward; others from hard compulsion, being required to leave friends and home, and all that they held dear, under the terror of a stern and despotic edict which they dared not disobey. It was even dangerous to ask for exemption.

As an instance of this, it is said that there was a Persian named Oebazus, who had three sons that had been drafted into the army. Oebazus, desirous of not being left wholly alone in his old age, made a request to the king that he would allow one of the sons to remain at home with his father. Darius appeared to receive this petition favorably. He told Oebazus that the request was so very modest and considerate that he would grant more than he asked. He would allow all three of his sons to remain with him. Oebazus retired from the king's presence overjoyed at the thought that his family was not to be separated at all. Darius ordered his guards to kill the three young men, and to send the dead bodies home, with a message to their father that his sons were restored to him, released forever from all obligation to serve the king.

The place of general rendezvous for the various forces which were to join in the expedition, consisting of the army which marched with Darius from Susa, and also of the troops and ships which the maritime provinces of Asia Minor were to supply on the way, was on the shores of the Bosporus, at the point where Mandrocles had constructed the bridge.[G] The people of Ionia, a region situated in Asia Minor, on the shores of the 夾 ean Sea, had been ordered to furnish a fleet of galleys, which they were to build and equip, and then send to the bridge. The destination of this fleet was to the Danube. It was to pass up the Bosporus into the Euxine Sea, now called the Black Sea, and thence into the mouth of the river. After ascending the Danube to a certain point, the men were to land and build a bridge across that river, using, very probably, their galleys for this purpose. In the mean time, the army was to cross the Bosporus by the bridge which had been erected there by Mandrocles, and pursue their way toward the Danube by land, through the kingdom of Thrace. By this arrangement, it was supposed that the bridge across the Danube would be ready by the time that the main body of the army arrived on the banks of the river. The idea of thus building in Asia Minor a bridge for the Danube, in the form of a vast fleet of galleys, to be sent round through the Black Sea to the mouths of the river, and thence up the river to its place of destination, was original and grand. It strikingly marks the military genius and skill which gave the Greeks so extended a fame, for it was by the Greeks that the exploit was to be performed.

[Footnote G: For the track of Darius on this expedition, see the map at the commencement of this volume.]

Darius marched magnificently through Asia Minor, on his way to the Bosporus, at the head of an army of seventy thousand men. He moved slowly, and the engineers and architects that accompanied him built columns and monuments here and there, as he advanced, to commemorate his progress. These structures were covered with inscriptions, which ascribed to Darius, as the leader of the enterprise, the most extravagant praise. At length the splendid array arrived at the place of rendezvous on the Bosporus, where there was soon presented to view a very grand and imposing scene.

The bridge of boats was completed, and the Ionian fleet, consisting of six hundred galleys, was at anchor near it in the stream. Long lines of tents were pitched upon the shore, and thousands of horsemen and of foot soldiers were drawn up in array, their banners flying, and their armor glittering in the sun, and all eager to see and to welcome the illustrious sovereign who had come, with so much pomp and splendor, to take them under his command. The banks of the Bosporus were picturesque and high, and all the eminences were crowded with spectators, to witness the imposing magnificence of the spectacle.

Darius encamped his army on the shore, and began to make the preparations necessary for the final departure of the expedition. He had been thus far within his own dominions. He was now, however, to pass into another quarter of the globe, to plunge into new and unknown dangers, among hostile, savage, and ferocious tribes. It was right that he should pause until he had considered well his plans, and secured attention to every point which could influence success.

He first examined the bridge of boats. He was very much pleased with the construction of it. He commended Mandrocles for his skill and fidelity in the highest terms, and loaded him with rewards and honors. Mandrocles used the money which Darius thus gave him in employing an artist to form a piece of statuary which should at once commemorate the building of the bridge and give to Darius the glory of it. The group represented the Bosporus with the bridge thrown over it, and the king on his throne reviewing his troops as they passed over the structure. This statuary was placed, when finished, in a temple in Greece, where it was universally admired. Darius was very much pleased both with the idea of this sculpture on the part of Mandrocles, and with the execution of it by the artist. He gave the bridge builder new rewards; he recompensed the artist, also, with similar munificence. He was pleased that they had contrived so happy a way of at the same time commemorating the bridging of the Bosporus and rendering exalted honor to him.

The bridge was situated about the middle of the Bosporus; and as the strait itself is about eighteen miles long, it was nine miles from the bridge to the Euxine Sea. There is a small group of islands near the mouth of this strait, where it opens into the sea, which were called in those days the Cyanean Islands. They were famed in the time of Darius for having once been floating islands, and enchanted. Their supernatural properties had disappeared, but there was one attraction which still pertained to them. They were situated beyond the limits of the strait, and the visitor who landed upon them could take his station on some picturesque cliff or smiling hill, and extend his view far and wide over the blue waters of the Euxine Sea.

Darius determined to make an excursion to these islands while the fleet and the army were completing their preparations at the bridge. He embarked, accordingly, on board a splendid galley, and, sailing along the Bosporus till he reached the sea, he landed on one of the islands. There was a temple there, consecrated to one of the Grecian deities. Darius, accompanied by his attendants and followers, ascended to this temple, and, taking a seat which had been provided for him there, he surveyed the broad expanse of water which extended like an ocean before him, and contemplated the grandeur of the scene with the greatest admiration and delight.

At length he returned to the bridge, where he found the preparations for the movement of the fleet and of the army nearly completed. He determined, before leaving the Asiatic shores, to erect a monument to commemorate his expedition, on the spot from which he was to take his final departure. He accordingly directed two columns of white marble to be reared, and inscriptions to be cut upon them, giving such particulars in respect to the expedition as it was desirable thus to preserve. These inscriptions contained his own name in very conspicuous characters as the leader of the enterprise; also an enumeration of the various nations that had contributed to form his army, with the numbers which each had furnished. There was a record of corresponding particulars, too, in respect to the fleet. The inscriptions were the same upon the two columns, except that upon the one it was written in the Assyrian tongue, which was the general language of the Persian empire, and upon the other in the Greek. Thus the two monuments were intended, the one for the Asiatic, and the other for the European world.

At length the day of departure arrived. The fleet set sail, and the immense train of the army put itself in motion to cross the bridge.[H] The fleet went on through the Bosporus to the Euxine, and thence along the western coast of that sea till it reached the mouths of the Danube. The ships entered the river by one of the branches which form the delta of the stream, and ascended for two days. This carried them above the ramifications into which the river divides itself at its mouth, to a spot where the current was confined to a single channel, and where the banks were firm. Here they landed, and while one part of the force which they had brought were occupied in organizing guards and providing defenses to protect the ground, the remainder commenced the work of arranging the vessels of the fleet, side by side, across the stream, to form the bridge.

[Footnote H: See Frontispiece.]

In the mean time, Darius, leading the great body of the army, advanced from the Bosporus by land. The country which the troops thus traversed was Thrace. They met with various adventures as they proceeded, and saw, as the accounts of the expedition state, many strange and marvelous phenomena. They came, for example, to the sources of a very wonderful river, which flows west and south toward the Aegean Sea. The name of the river was the Tearus. It came from thirty-eight springs, all issuing from the same rock, some hot and some cold. The waters of the stream which was produced by the mingling of these fountains were pure, limpid, and delicious, and were possessed of remarkable medicinal properties, being efficacious for the cure of various diseases. Darius was so much pleased with this river, that his army halted to refresh themselves with its waters, and he caused one of his monuments to be erected on the spot, the inscription of which contained not only the usual memorials of the march, but also a tribute to the salubrity of the waters of this magical stream.

At one point in the course of the march through Thrace, Darius conceived the idea of varying the construction of his line of monuments by building a cairn. A cairn is a heap of stones, such as is reared in the mountains of Scotland and of Switzerland by the voluntary additions of every passer by, to commemorate a spot marked as the scene of some accident or disaster. As each guide finishes the story of the incident in the hearing of the party which he conducts, each tourist who has listened to it adds his stone to the heap, until the rude structure attains sometimes to a very considerable size. Darius, fixing upon a suitable spot near one of his encampments, commanded every soldier in the army to bring a stone and place it on the pile. A vast mound rose rapidly from these contributions, which, when completed, not only commemorated the march of the army, but denoted, also, by the immense number of the stones entering into the composition of the pile, the countless multitude of soldiers that formed the expedition.

There was a story told to Darius, as he was traversing these regions, of a certain king, reigning over some one of the nations that occupied them, who wished to make an enumeration of the inhabitants of his realm. The mode which he adopted was to require every man in his dominions to send him an arrow head. When all the arrow heads were in, the vast collection was counted by the official arithmeticians, and the total of the population was thus attained. The arrow heads were then laid together in a sort of monumental pile. It was, perhaps, this primitive mode of census-taking which suggested to Darius the idea of his cairn.

There was a tribe of barbarians through whose dominions Darius passed on his way from the Bosporus to the Danube, that observed a custom in their religious worship, which, though in itself of a shocking character, suggests reflections of salutary influence for our own minds. There is a universal instinct in the human heart, leading it strongly to feel the need of help from an unseen and supernatural world in its sorrows and trials; and it is almost always the case that rude and savage nations, in their attempts to obtain this spiritual aid, connect the idea of personal privation and suffering on their part, self inflicted if necessary, as a means of seeking it. It seems as if the instinctive conviction of personal guilt, which associates itself so naturally and so strongly in the minds of men with all conceptions of the unseen world and of divine power, demands something like an expiation as an essential prerequisite to obtaining audience and acceptance with the King of Heaven. The tribe of savages above referred to manifested this feeling by a dreadful observance. Once in every five years they were accustomed to choose by lot, with solemn ceremonies, one of their number, to be sent as a legate or embassador to their god. The victim, when chosen, was laid down upon the ground in the midst of the vast assembly convened to witness the rite, while officers designated for the purpose stood by, armed with javelins. Other men, selected for their great personal strength, then took the man from the ground by the hands and feet, and swinging him to and fro three times to gain momentum, they threw him with all their force into the air, and the armed men, when he came down, caught him on the points of their javelins. If he was killed by this dreadful impalement, all was right. He would bear the message of the wants and necessities of the tribe to their god, and they might reasonably expect a favorable reception. If, on the other hand, he did not die, he was thought to be rejected by the god as a wicked man and an unsuitable messenger. The unfortunate convalescent was, in such cases, dismissed in disgrace, and another messenger chosen.

The army of Darius reached the banks of the Danube at last, and they found that the fleet of the Ionians had attained the point agreed upon before them, and were awaiting their arrival. The vessels were soon arranged in the form of a bridge across the stream, and as there was no enemy at hand to embarrass them, the army soon accomplished the passage. They were now fairly in the Scythian country, and immediately began their preparations to advance and meet the foe. Darius gave orders to have the bridge broken up, and the galleys abandoned and destroyed, as he chose rather to take with him the whole of his force, than to leave a guard behind sufficient to protect this shipping. These orders were about to be executed, when a Grecian general, who was attached to one of the bodies of troops which were furnished from the provinces of Asia Minor, asked leave to speak to the king. The king granted him an audience, when he expressed his opinion as follows:

"It seems to me to be more prudent, sire, to leave the bridge as it is, under the care of those who have constructed it, as it may be that we shall have occasion to use it on our return. I do not recommend the preservation of it as a means of securing a retreat, for, in case we meet the Scythians at all, I am confident of victory; but our enemy consists of wandering hordes who have no fixed habitation, and their country is entirely without cities or posts of any kind which they will feel any strong interest in defending, and thus it is possible that we may not be able to find any enemy to combat. Besides, if we succeed in our enterprise as completely as we can desire, it will be important, on many accounts, to preserve an open and free communication with the countries behind us."

The king approved of this counsel, and countermanded his orders for the destruction of the bridge. He directed that the Ionian forces that had accompanied the fleet should remain at the river to guard the bridge. They were to remain thus on guard for two months, and then, if Darius did not return, and if they heard no tidings of him, they were at liberty to leave their post, and to go back, with their galleys, to their own land again.

Two months would seem to be a very short time to await the return of an army going on such an expedition into boundless and trackless wilds. There can, however, scarcely be any accidental error in the statement of the time, as the mode which Darius adopted to enable the guard thus left at the bridge to keep their reckoning was a very singular one, and it is very particularly described. He took a cord, it is said, and tied sixty knots in it. This cord he delivered to the Ionian chiefs who were to be left in charge of the bridge, directing them to untie one of the knots every day. When the cord should become, by this process, wholly free, the detachment were also at liberty. They might thereafter, at any time, abandon the post intrusted to them, and return to their homes.

We can not suppose that military men, capable of organizing a force of seventy thousand troops for so distant an expedition, and possessed of sufficient science and skill to bridge the Bosporus and the Danube, could have been under any necessity of adopting so childish a method as this as a real reliance in regulating their operations. It must be recollected, however, that, though the commanders in these ancient days were intelligent and strong-minded men, the common soldiers were but children both in intellect and in ideas; and it was the custom of all great commanders to employ outward and visible symbols to influence and govern them. The sense of loneliness and desertion which such soldiers would naturally feel in being left in solitude on the banks of the river, would be much diminished by seeing before them a marked and definite termination to the period of their stay, and to have, in the cord hanging up in their camp, a visible token that the remnant of time that remained was steadily diminishing day by day; while, in the mean time, Darius was fully determined that, long before the knots should be all untied, he would return to the river.

CHAPTER IX.

THE RETREAT FROM SCYTHIA.

B.C. 513

Motive for Darius's invasion.--The foundation of government.--Darius without justification in invading Scythia.--Alarm of the Scythians.--Condition of the tribes.--Men metamorphosed into wolves.--Story of the Amazons.--Adventures of the Amazons.--Two of them captured.--The corps of cavaliers.--Their maneuvers.--Success of the cavaliers.--Matrimonial alliances.--The Amazons rule their husbands.--They establish a separate tribe.--The Scythians send an embassy to the neighboring tribes.--Habits of the Scythians.--Their mode of warfare.--Message to Indathyrsus.--His reply.--The Scythian cavalry.--Their attacks on the Persians.--Braying of the Persian asses.--Scythians sent to the bridge.--Agreement with the Ionians.--The Scythians change their policy.--The Scythians' strange presents.--Various interpretations.--Opinions of the Persian officers.--The Scythians draw up their forces.--The armies prepare for battle.--Hunting the hare.--The Persians resolve to retreat.--Stratagem and secret flight.--Surrender of the camp.--Difficulties of the retreat.--The bridge partially destroyed.--Darius arrives at the Danube.--The bridge repaired.--The army returns to Asia.

The motive which dictated Darius's invasion of Scythia seems to have been purely a selfish and domineering love of power. The attempts of a stronger and more highly civilized state to extend its dominion over a weaker and more lawless one, are not, however, necessarily and always of this character.

Divine Providence, in making men gregarious in nature, has given them an instinct of organization, which is as intrinsic and as essential a characteristic of the human soul as maternal love or the principle of self-preservation. The right, therefore, of organizations of men to establish law and order among themselves, and to extend these principles to other communities around them, so far as such interpositions are really promotive of the interests and welfare of those affected by them, rests on precisely the same foundation as the right of the father to govern the child. This foundation is the existence and universality of an instinctive principle implanted by the Creator in the human heart; a principle which we are bound to submit to, both because it is a fundamental and constituent element in the very structure of man, and because its recognition and the acknowledgment of its authority are absolutely essential to his continued existence. Wherever law and order, therefore, among men do not exist, it may be properly established and enforced by any neighboring organization that has power to do it, just as wherever there is a group of children they may be justly controlled and governed by their father. It seems equally unnecessary to invent a fictitious and wholly imaginary compact to justify the jurisdiction in the one case as in the other.

If the Scythians, therefore, had been in a state of confusion and anarchy, Darius might justly have extended his own well-regulated and settled government over them, and, in so doing, would have promoted the general good of mankind. But he had no such design. It was a desire for personal aggrandizement, and a love of fame and power, which prompted him. He offered it as a pretext to justify his invasion, that the Scythians, in former years, had made incursions into the Persian dominions; but this was only a pretext. The expedition was a wanton attack upon neighbors whom he supposed unable to resist him, simply for the purpose of adding to his own already gigantic power.

When Darius commenced his march from the river, the Scythians had heard rumors of his approach. They sent, as soon as they were aware of the impending danger, to all the nations and tribes around them, in order to secure their alliance and aid. These people were all wandering and half-savage tribes, like the Scythians themselves, though each seems to have possessed its own special and distinctive mark of barbarity. One tribe were accustomed to carry home the heads of the enemies which they had slain in battle, and each one, impaling his own dreadful trophy upon a stake, would set it up upon his house-top, over the chimney, where they imagined that it would have the effect of a charm, and serve as a protection for the family. Another tribe lived in habits of promiscuous intercourse, like the lower orders of animals; and so, as the historian absurdly states, being, in consequence of this mode of life, all connected together by the ties of consanguinity, they lived in perpetual peace and good will, without any envy, or jealousy, or other evil passion. A third occupied a region so infested with serpents that they were once driven wholly out of the country by them. It was said of these people that, once in every year, they were all metamorphosed into wolves, and, after remaining for a few days in this form, they were transformed again into men. A fourth tribe painted their bodies blue and red, and a fifth were cannibals.

The most remarkable, however, of all the tales related about these northern savages was the story of the Sauromateans and their Amazonian wives. The Amazons were a nation of masculine and ferocious women, who often figure in ancient histories and legends. They rode on horseback astride like men, and their courage and strength in battle were such that scarcely any troops could subdue them. It happened, however, upon one time, that some Greeks conquered a body of them somewhere upon the shores of the Euxine Sea, and took a large number of them prisoners. They placed these prisoners on board of three ships, and put to sea. The Amazons rose upon their captors and threw them overboard, and thus obtained possession of the ships. They immediately proceeded toward the shore, and landed, not knowing where they were. It happened to be on the northwestern coast of the sea that they landed. Here they roamed up and down the country, until presently they fell in with a troop of horses. These they seized and mounted, arming themselves, at the same time, either with the weapons which they had procured on board the ships, or fabricated, themselves, on the shore. Thus organized and equipped, they began to make excursions for plunder, and soon became a most formidable band of marauders. The Scythians of the country supposed that they were men, but they could learn nothing certain respecting them. Their language, their appearance, their manners, and their dress were totally new, and the inhabitants were utterly unable to conceive who they were, and from what place they could so suddenly and mysteriously have come.

At last, in one of the encounters which took place, the Scythians took two of these strange invaders prisoners. To their utter amazement, they found that they were women. On making this discovery, they changed their mode of dealing with them, and resolved upon a plan based on the supposed universality of the instincts of their sex. They enlisted a corps of the most handsome and vigorous young men that could be obtained, and after giving them instructions, the nature of which will be learned by the result, they sent them forth to meet the Amazons.

The corps of Scythian cavaliers went out to seek their female antagonists with designs any thing but belligerent. They advanced to the encampment of the Amazons, and hovered about for some time in their vicinity, without, however, making any warlike demonstrations. They had been instructed to show themselves as much as possible to the enemy, but by no means to fight them. They would, accordingly, draw as near to the Amazons as was safe, and linger there, gazing upon them, as if under the influence of some sort of fascination. If the Amazons advanced toward them, they would fall back, and if the advance continued, they would retreat fast enough to keep effectually out of the way. Then, when the Amazons turned, they would turn too, follow them back, and linger near them, around their encampment, as before.

The Amazonians were for a time puzzled with this strange demeanor, and they gradually learned to look upon the handsome horsemen at first without fear, and finally even without hostility. At length, one day, one of the young horsemen, observing an Amazon who had strayed away from the rest, followed and joined her. She did not repel him. They were not able to converse together, as neither knew the language of the other. They established a friendly intercourse, however, by looks and signs, and after a time they separated, each agreeing to bring one of their companions to the place of rendezvous on the following day.

A friendly intercommunication being thus commenced, the example spread very rapidly; matrimonial alliances began to be formed, and, in a word, a short time only elapsed before the two camps were united and intermingled, the Scythians and the Amazons being all paired together in the most intimate relations of domestic life. Thus, true to the instincts of their sex, the rude and terrible maidens decided, when the alternative was fairly presented to them, in favor of husbands and homes, rather than continuing the life they had led, of independence, conflict, and plunder. It is curious to observe that the means by which they were won, namely, a persevering display of admiration and attentions, steadily continued, but not too eagerly and impatiently pressed, and varied with an adroit and artful alternation of advances and retreats, were precisely the same as those by which, in every age, the attempt is usually made to win the heart of woman from hatred and hostility to love.

We speak of the Amazonians as having been won; but they were, in fact, themselves the conquerors of their captors, after all; for it appeared, in the end, that in the future plans and arrangements of the united body, they ruled their Scythian husbands, and not the Scythians them. The husbands wished to return home with their wives, whom, they said, they would protect and maintain in the midst of their countrymen in honor and in peace. The Amazons, however, were in favor of another plan. Their habits and manners were such, they said, that they should not be respected and beloved among any other people. They wished that their husbands, therefore, would go home and settle their affairs, and afterward return and join their wives again, and then that all together should move to the eastward, until they should find a suitable place to settle in by themselves. This plan was acceded to by the husbands, and was carried into execution; and the result was the planting of a new nation, called the Sauromateans, who thenceforth took their place among the other barbarous tribes that dwelt upon the northern shores of the Euxine Sea.

Such was the character of the tribes and nations that dwelt in the neighborhood of the Scythian country. As soon as Darius had passed the river, the Scythians sent embassadors to all their people, proposing to them to form a general alliance against the invader. "We ought to make common cause against him," said they; "for if he subdues one nation, it will only open the way for an attack upon the rest. Some of us are, it is true, more remote than others from the immediate danger, but it threatens us all equally in the end."

The embassadors delivered their message, and some of the tribes acceded to the Scythian proposals. Others, however, refused. The quarrel, they said, was a quarrel between Darius and the Scythians alone, and they were not inclined to bring upon themselves the hostility of so powerful a sovereign by interfering. The Scythians were very indignant at this refusal; but there was no remedy, and they accordingly began to prepare to defend themselves as well as they could, with the help of those nations that had expressed a willingness to join them.

The habits of the Scythians were nomadic and wandering, and their country was one vast region of verdant and beautiful, and yet, in a great measure, of uncultivated and trackless wilds. They had few towns and villages, and those few were of little value. They adopted, therefore, the mode of warfare which, in such a country and for such a people, is always the wisest to be pursued. They retreated slowly before Darius's advancing army, carrying off or destroying all such property as might aid the king in respect to his supplies. They organized and equipped a body of swift horsemen, who were ordered to hover around Darius's camp, and bring intelligence to the Scythian generals of every movement. These horsemen, too, were to harass the flanks and the rear of the army, and to capture or destroy every man whom they should find straying away from the camp. By this means they kept the invading army continually on the alert, allowing them no peace and no repose, while yet they thwarted and counteracted all the plans and efforts which the enemy made to bring on a general battle.

As the Persians advanced in pursuit of the enemy, the Scythians retreated, and in this retreat they directed their course toward the countries occupied by those nations that had refused to join in the alliance. By this artful management they transferred the calamity and the burden of the war to the territories of their neighbors. Darius soon found that he was making no progress toward gaining his end. At length he concluded to try the effect of a direct and open challenge.

He accordingly sent embassadors to the Scythian chief, whose name was Indathyrsus, with a message somewhat as follows:

"Foolish man! how long will you continue to act in this absurd and preposterous manner? It is incumbent on you to make a decision in favor of one thing or the other. If you think that you are able to contend with me, stop, and let us engage. If not, then acknowledge me as your superior, and submit to my authority."

The Scythian chief sent back the following reply:

"We have no inducement to contend with you in open battle on the field, because you are not doing us any injury, nor is it at present in your power to do us any. We have no cities and no cultivated fields that you can seize or plunder. Your roaming about our country, therefore, does us no harm, and you are at liberty to continue it as long as it gives you any pleasure. There is nothing on our soil that you can injure, except one spot, and that is the place where the sepulchres of our fathers lie. If you were to attack that spot--which you may perhaps do, if you can find it--you may rely upon a battle. In the mean time, you may go elsewhere, wherever you please. As to acknowledging your superiority, we shall do nothing of the kind. We defy you."

Notwithstanding the refusal of the Scythians to give the Persians battle, they yet made, from time to time, partial and unexpected onsets upon their camp, seizing occasions when they hoped to find their enemies off their guard. The Scythians had troops of cavalry which were very efficient and successful in these attacks. These horsemen were, however, sometimes thrown into confusion and driven back by a very singular means of defense. It seems that the Persians had brought with them from Europe, in their train, a great number of asses, as beasts of burden, to transport the tents and the baggage of the army. These asses were accustomed, in times of excitement and danger, to set up a very terrific braying. It was, in fact, all that they could do. Braying at a danger seems to be a very ridiculous mode of attempting to avert it, but it was a tolerably effectual mode, nevertheless, in this case at least; for the Scythian horses, who would have faced spears and javelins, and the loudest shouts and vociferations of human adversaries without any fear, were appalled and put to flight at hearing the unearthly noises which issued from the Persian camp whenever they approached it. Thus the mighty monarch of the whole Asiatic world seemed to depend for protection against the onsets of these rude and savage troops on the braying of his asses!

* * * * *

While these things were going on in the interior of the country, the Scythians sent down a detachment of their forces to the banks of the Danube, to see if they could not, in some way or other, obtain possession of the bridge. They learned here what the orders were which Darius had given to the

Ionians who had been left in charge, in respect to the time of their remaining at their post. The Scythians told them that if they would govern themselves strictly by those orders, and so break up the bridge and go down the river with their boats as soon as the two months should have expired, they should not be molested in the mean time. The Ionians agreed to this. The time was then already nearly gone, and they promised that, so soon as it should be fully expired, they would withdraw.

The Scythian detachment sent back word to the main army acquainting them with these facts, and the army accordingly resolved on a change in their policy. Instead of harassing and distressing the Persians as they had done, to hasten their departure, they now determined to improve the situation of their enemies, and encourage them in their hopes, so as to protract their stay. They accordingly allowed the Persians to gain the advantage over them in small skirmishes, and they managed, also, to have droves of cattle fall into their hands, from time to time, so as to supply them with food. The Persians were quite elated with these indications that the tide of fortune was about to turn in their favor.

While things were in this state, there appeared one day at the Persian camp a messenger from the Scythians, who said that he had some presents from the Scythian chief for Darius. The messenger was admitted, and allowed to deliver his gifts. The gifts proved to be a bird, a mouse, a frog, and five arrows. The Persians asked the bearer of these strange offerings what the Scythians meant by them. He replied that he had no explanations to give. His orders were, he said, to deliver the presents and then return; and that they must, accordingly, find out the meaning intended by the exercise of their own ingenuity.

When the messenger had retired, Darius and the Persians consulted together, to determine what so strange a communication could mean. They could not, however, come to any satisfactory decision. Darius said that he thought the three animals might probably be intended to denote the three kingdoms of nature to which the said animals respectively belonged, viz., the earth, the air, and the water; and as the giving up of weapons was a token of submission, the whole might mean that the Scythians were now ready to give up the contest, and acknowledge the right of the Persians to supreme and universal dominion.

The officers, however, did not generally concur in this opinion. They saw no indications, they said, of any disposition on the part of the Scythians to surrender. They thought it quite as probable that the communication was meant to announce to those who received it threats and defiance, as to express conciliation and submission. "It may mean," said one of them, "that, unless you can fly like a bird into the air, or hide like a mouse in the ground, or bury yourselves, like the frog, in morasses and fens, you can not escape our arrows."

There was no means of deciding positively between these contradictory interpretations, but it soon became evident that the former of the two was very far from being correct; for, soon after the present was received, the Scythians were seen to be drawing up their forces in array, as if preparing for battle. The two months had expired, and they had reason to suppose that the party at the bridge had withdrawn, as they had promised to do. Darius had been so far weakened by his harassing marches, and the manifold privations and sufferings of his men, that he felt some solicitude in respect to the result of a battle, now that it seemed to be drawing near, although such a trial of strength had been the object which he had been, from the beginning, most eager to secure.

The two armies were encamped at a moderate distance from each other, with a plain, partly wooded, between them. While in this position, and before any hostile action was commenced by either party, it was observed from the camp of Darius that suddenly a great tumult arose from the Scythian lines. Men were seen rushing in dense crowds this way and that over the plain, with shouts and outcries, which, however, had in them no expression of anger or fear, but rather one of gayety and pleasure. Darius demanded what the strange tumult meant. Some messengers were sent out to ascertain the cause, and on their return they reported that the Scythians were hunting a hare, which had suddenly made its appearance. The hare had issued from a thicket, and a considerable portion of the army, officers and soldiers, had abandoned their ranks to enjoy the sport of pursuing it, and were running impetuously, here and there, across the plain, filling the air with shouts of hilarity.

"They do indeed despise us," said Darius, "since, on the eve of a battle, they can lose all thoughts of us and of their danger, and abandon their posts to hunt a hare!"

That evening a council of war was held. It was concluded that the Scythians must be very confident and strong in their position, and that, if a general battle were to be hazarded, it would be very doubtful what would be the result. The Persians concluded unanimously, therefore, that the wisest plan would be for them to give up the intended conquest, and retire from the country. Darius accordingly proceeded to make his preparations for a secret retreat.

He separated all the infirm and feeble portion of the army from the rest, and informed them that he was going that night on a short expedition with the main body of the troops, and that, while he was gone, they were to remain and defend the camp. He ordered the men to build the camp fires, and to make them larger and more numerous than common, and then had the asses tied together in an unusual situation, so that they should keep up a continual braying. These sounds, heard all the night, and the light of the camp fires, were to lead the Scythians to believe that the whole body of the Persians remained, as usual, at the encampment, and thus to prevent all suspicion of their flight.

Toward midnight, Darius marched forth in silence and secrecy, with all the vigorous and able-bodied forces under his command, leaving the weary, the sick, and the infirm to the mercy of their enemies. The long column succeeded in making good their retreat, without exciting the suspicions of the Scythians. They took the route which they supposed would conduct them most directly to the river.

When the troops which remained in the camp found, on the following morning, that they had been deceived and abandoned, they made signals to the Scythians to come to them, and, when they came, the invalids surrendered themselves and the camp to their possession. The Scythians then, immediately, leaving a proper guard to defend the camp, set out to follow the Persian army. Instead, however, of keeping directly upon their track, they took a shorter course, which would lead them more speedily to the river. The Persians, being unacquainted with the country, got involved in fens and morasses, and other difficulties of the way, and their progress was thus so much impeded that the Scythians reached the river before them.

They found the Ionians still there, although the two months had fully expired. It is possible that the chiefs had received secret orders from Darius not to hasten their departure, even after the knots had all been untied; or perhaps they chose, of their own accord, to await their sovereign's return. The Scythians immediately urged them to be gone. "The time has expired," they said, "and you are no longer under any obligation to wait. Return to your own country, and assert your own independence and freedom, which you can safely do if you leave Darius and his armies here."

The Ionians consulted together on the subject, doubtful, at first, what to do. They concluded that they would not comply with the Scythian proposals, while yet they determined to pretend to comply with them, in order to avoid the danger of being attacked. They accordingly began to take the bridge to pieces, commencing on the Scythian side of the stream. The Scythians, seeing the work thus going on, left the ground, and marched back to meet the Persians. The armies, however, fortunately for Darius, missed each other, and the Persians arrived safely at the river, after the Scythians had left it. They arrived in the night, and the advanced guard, seeing no appearance of the bridge on the Scythian side, supposed that the Ionians had gone. They shouted long and loud on the shore, and at length an Egyptian, who was celebrated for the power of his voice, succeeded in making the Ionians hear. The boats were immediately brought back to their positions, the bridge was reconstructed, and Darius's army recrossed the stream.

The Danube being thus safely crossed, the army made the best of its way back through Thrace, and across the Bosporus into Asia, and thus ended Darius's great expedition against the Scythians.

CHAPTER X.

THE STORY OF HISTIS.

B.C. 504

The nature of the government which was exercised in ancient times by a royal despot like Darius, and the character of the measures and management to which he was accustomed to resort to gain his political ends, are, in many points, very strikingly illustrated by the story of Histis.

Histis was the Ionian chieftain who had been left in charge of the bridge of boats across the Danube when Darius made his incursion into Scythia. When, on the failure of the expedition, Darius returned to the river, knowing, as he did, that the two months had expired, he naturally felt a considerable degree of solicitude lest he should find the bridge broken up and the vessels gone, in which case his situation would be very desperate, hemmed in, as he would have been, between the Scythians and the river. His anxiety was changed into terror when his advanced guard arrived at the bank and found that no signs of the bridge were to be seen. It is easy to imagine what, under these circumstances, must have been the relief and joy of all the army, when they heard friendly answers to their shouts, coming, through the darkness of the night, over the waters of the river, assuring them that their faithful allies were still at their posts, and that they themselves would soon be in safety.

Darius, though he was governed by no firm and steady principles of justice, was still a man of many generous impulses. He was grateful for favors, though somewhat capricious in his modes of requiting them. He declared to Histis that he felt under infinite obligations to him for his persevering fidelity, and that, as soon as the army should have safely arrived in Asia, he would confer upon him such rewards as would evince the reality of his gratitude.

On his return from Scythia, Darius brought back the whole of his army over the Danube, thus abandoning entirely the country of the Scythians; but he did not transport the whole body across the Bosporus. He left a considerable detachment of troops, under the command of one of his generals, named Megabyzus, in Thrace, on the European side, ordering Megabyzus to establish himself there, and to reduce all the countries in that neighborhood to his sway. Darius then proceeded to Sardis, which was the most powerful and wealthy of his capitals in that quarter of the world. At Sardis, he was, as it were, at home again, and he accordingly took an early opportunity to send for Histis, as well as some others who had rendered him special services in his late campaign, in order that he might agree with them in respect to their reward. He asked Histis what favor he wished to receive.

Histis replied that he was satisfied, on the whole, with the position which he already enjoyed, which was that of king or governor of Miletus, an Ionian city, south of Sardis, and on the shores of the Aegean Sea.[I] He should be pleased, however, he said, if the king would assign him a certain small territory in Thrace, or, rather, on the borders between Thrace and Macedonia, near the mouth of the River Strymon. He wished to build a city there. The king immediately granted this request, which was obviously very moderate and reasonable. He did not, perhaps, consider that this territory, being in Thrace, or in its immediate vicinity, came within the jurisdiction of Megabyzus, whom he had left in command there, and that the grant might lead to some conflict between the two generals. There was special danger of jealousy and disagreement between them, for Megabyzus was a Persian, and Histis was a Greek.

[Footnote I: For these places, see the map at the commencement of the next chapter.]

Histis organized a colony, and, leaving a temporary and provisional government at Miletus, he proceeded along the shores of the Aegean Sea to the spot assigned him, and began to build his city. As the locality was beyond the Thracian frontier, and at a considerable distance from the head-quarters of Megabyzus, it is very probable that the operations of Histis would not have attracted the Persian general's attention for a considerable time, had it not been for a very extraordinary and peculiar train of circumstances, which led him to discover them. The circumstances were these:

There was a nation or tribe called the Peonians, who inhabited the valley of the Strymon, which river came down from the interior of the country, and fell into the sea near the place where Histis was building his city. Among the Peonian chieftains there were two who wished to obtain the government of the country, but they were not quite strong enough to effect their object. In order to weaken the force which was opposed to them, they conceived the base design of betraying their tribe to Darius, and inducing him to make them captives. If their plan should succeed, a considerable portion of the population would be taken away, and they could easily, they supposed, obtain ascendency over the rest. In order to call the attention of Darius to the subject, and induce him to act as they desired, they resorted to the following stratagem. Their object seems to have been to lead Darius to undertake a campaign against their countrymen, by showing him what excellent and valuable slaves they would make.

These two chieftains were brothers, and they had a very beautiful sister; her form was graceful and elegant, and her countenance lovely. They brought this sister with them to Sardis when Darius was there. They dressed and decorated her in a very careful manner, but yet in a style appropriate to the condition of a servant; and then, one day, when the king was sitting in some public place in the city, as was customary with Oriental sovereigns, they sent her to pass along the street before him, equipped in such a manner as to show that she was engaged in servile occupations. She had a jar, such as was then used for carrying water, poised upon her head, and she was leading a horse by means of a bridle hung over her arm. Her hands, being thus not required either for the horse or for the vessel, were employed in spinning, as she walked along, by means of a distaff and spindle.

The attention of Darius was strongly attracted to the spectacle. The beauty of the maiden, the novelty and strangeness of her costume, the multiplicity of her avocations, and the ease and grace with which she performed them, all conspired to awaken the monarch's curiosity. He directed one of his attendants to follow her and see where she should go. The attendant did so. The girl went to the river. She watered her horse, filled her jar and placed it on her head, and then, hanging the bridle on her arm again, she returned through the same streets, and passed the king's palace as before, spinning as she walked along.

The interest and curiosity of the king was excited more than ever by the reappearance of the girl and by the report of his messenger. He directed that she should be stopped and brought into his presence. She came; and her brothers, who had been watching the whole scene from a convenient spot near at hand, joined her and came too. The king asked them who they were. They replied that they were Peonians. He wished to know where they lived. "On the banks of the River Strymon," they replied, "near the confines of Thrace." He next asked whether all the women of their country were accustomed to labor, and were as ingenious, and dexterous, and beautiful as their sister. The brothers replied that they were.

Darius immediately determined to make the whole people slaves. He accordingly dispatched a courier with the orders. The courier crossed the

Hellespont, and proceeded to the encampment of Megabyzus in Thrace. He delivered his dispatches to the Persian general, commanding him to proceed immediately to Peonia, and there to take the whole community prisoners, and bring them to Darius in Sardis. Megabyzus, until this time, had known nothing of the people whom he was thus commanded to seize. He, however, found some Thracian guides who undertook to conduct him to their territory; and then, taking with him a sufficient force, he set out on the expedition. The Peonians heard of his approach. Some prepared to defend themselves; others fled to the mountains. The fugitives escaped, but those who attempted to resist were taken. Megabyzus collected the unfortunate captives, together with their wives and children, and brought them down to the coast to embark them for Sardis. In doing this, he had occasion to pass by the spot where Histis was building his city, and it was then, for the first time, that Megabyzus became acquainted with the plan. Histis was building a wall to defend his little territory on the side of the land. Ships and galleys were going and coming on the side of the sea. Every thing indicated that the work was rapidly and prosperously advancing.

Megabyzus did not interfere with the work; but, as soon as he arrived at Sardis with his captives, and had delivered them to the king, he introduced the subject of Histis's city, and represented to Darius that it would be dangerous to the Persian interests to allow such an enterprise to go on. "He will establish a strong post there," said Megabyzus, "by means of which he will exercise a great ascendency over all the neighboring seas. The place is admirably situated for a naval station, as the country in the vicinity abounds with all the materials for building and equipping ships. There are also mines of silver in the mountains near, from which he will obtain a great supply of treasure. By these means he will become so strong in a short period of time, that, after you have returned to Asia, he will revolt from your authority, carrying with him, perhaps, in his rebellion, all the Greeks of Asia Minor."

The king said that he was sorry that he had made the grant, and that he would revoke it without delay.

Megabyzus recommended that the king should not do this in an open or violent manner, but that he should contrive some way to arrest the progress of the undertaking without any appearance of suspicion or displeasure.

Darius accordingly sent for Histis to come to him at Sardis, saying that there was a service of great importance on which he wished to employ him. Histis, of course, obeyed such a summons with eager alacrity. When he arrived, Darius expressed great pleasure at seeing him once more, and said that he had constant need of his presence and his counsels. He valued, above all price, the services of so faithful a friend, and so sagacious and trusty an adviser. He was now, he said, going to Susa, and he wished Histis to accompany him as his privy counselor and confidential friend. It would be necessary, Darius added, that he should give up his government of Miletus, and also the city in Thrace which he had begun to build; but he should be exalted to higher honors and dignities at Susa in their stead. He should have apartments in the king's palace, and live in great luxury and splendor.

Histis was extremely disappointed and chagrined at this announcement. He was obliged, however, to conceal his vexation and submit to his fate. In a few days after this, he set out, with the rest of Darius's court, for the Persian capital, leaving a nephew, whose name was Aristagoras, as governor of Miletus in his stead. Darius, on the other hand, committed the general charge of the whole coast of Asia Minor to Artaphernes, one of his generals. Artaphernes was to make Sardis his capital. He had not only the general command of all the provinces extending along the shore, but also of all the ships, and galleys, and other naval armaments which belonged to Darius on the neighboring seas. Aristagoras, as governor of Miletus, was under his general jurisdiction. The two officers were, moreover, excellent friends. Aristagoras was, of course, a Greek, and Artaphernes a Persian.

Among the Greek islands situated in the Aegean Sea, one of the most wealthy, important, and powerful at that time, was Naxos. It was situated in the southern part of the sea, and about midway between the shores of Asia Minor and Greece. It happened that, soon after Darius had returned from Asia Minor to Persia, a civil war broke out in that island, in which the common people were on one side and the nobles on the other. The nobles were overcome in the contest, and fled from the island. A party of them landed at Miletus, and called upon Aristagoras to aid them in regaining possession of the island.

Aristagoras replied that he would very gladly do it if he had the power, but that the Persian forces on the whole coast, both naval and military, were under the command of Artaphernes at Sardis. He said, however, that he was on very friendly terms with Artaphernes, and that he would, if the Naxians desired it, apply to him for his aid. The Naxians seemed very grateful for the interest which Aristagoras took in their cause, and said that they would commit the whole affair to his charge.

There was, however, much less occasion for gratitude than there seemed, for Aristagoras was very far from being honest and sincere in his offers of aid. He perceived, immediately on hearing the fugitives' story, that a very favorable opportunity was opening for him to add Naxos, and perhaps even the neighboring islands, to his own government. It is always a favorable opportunity to subjugate a people when their power of defense and of resistance is neutralized by dissensions with one another. It is a device as old as the history of mankind, and one resorted to now as often as ever, for ambitious neighbors to interpose in behalf of the weaker party, in a civil war waged in a country which they wish to make their own, and, beginning with a war against a part, to end by subjugating the whole. This was Aristagoras's plan. He proposed it to Artaphernes, representing to him that a very favorable occasion had occurred for bringing the Greek islands of the 荧 ean Sea under the Persian dominion. Naxos once possessed, all the other islands around it would follow, he said, and a hundred ships would make the conquest sure.

Artaphernes entered very readily and very warmly into the plan. He said that he would furnish two hundred instead of one hundred galleys. He thought it was necessary, however, first to consult Darius, since the affair was one of such importance; and besides, it was not best to commence the undertaking until the spring. He would immediately send a messenger to Darius to ascertain his pleasure, and, in the mean time, as he did not doubt that Darius would fully approve of the plan, he would have all necessary preparations made, so that every thing should be in readiness as soon as the proper season for active operations should arrive.

Artaphernes was right in anticipating his brother's approval of the design. The messenger returned from Susa with full authority from the king for the execution of the project. The ships were built and equipped, and every thing was made ready for the expedition. The intended destination of the armament was, however, kept a profound secret, as the invaders wished to surprise the people of Naxos when off their guard. Aristagoras was to accompany the expedition as its general leader, while an officer named Megabates, appointed by Artaphernes for this purpose, was to take command of the fleet as a sort of admiral. Thus there were two commanders--an arrangement which almost always, in such cases, leads to a quarrel. It is a maxim in war that one bad general is better than two good ones.

The expedition sailed from Miletus; and, in order to prevent the people of Naxos from being apprised of their danger, the report had been circulated that its destination was to be the Hellespont. Accordingly, when the fleet sailed, it turned its course to the northward, as if it were really going to the Hellespont. The plan of the commander was to stop after proceeding a short distance, and then to seize the first opportunity afforded by a wind from the north to come down suddenly upon Naxos, before the population should have time to prepare for defense. Accordingly, when they arrived opposite the island of Chios, the whole fleet came to anchor near the land. The ships were all ordered to be ready, at a moment's warning, for setting sail; and, thus situated, the commanders were waiting for the wind to change.

Megabates, in going his rounds among the fleet while things were in this condition, found one vessel entirely abandoned. The captain and crew had all left it, and had gone ashore. They were not aware, probably, how urgent was the necessity that they should be every moment at their posts. The captain of this galley was a native of a small town called Cnydus, and, as it happened, was a particular friend of Aristagoras. His name was Syclax. Megabates, as the commander of the fleet, was very much incensed at finding one of his subordinate officers so derelict in duty. He sent his guards in pursuit of him; and when Syclax was brought to his ship, Megabates ordered his head to be thrust out through one of the small port-holes intended for the oars, in the side of the ship, and then bound him in that position--his head appearing thus to view, in the sight of all the fleet, while his body remained within the vessel. "I am going to keep him at his post," said Megabates, "and in such a way that every one can see that he is there."

Aristagoras was much distressed at seeing his friend suffering so severe and disgraceful a punishment. He went to Megabates and requested the release of the prisoner, giving, at the same time, what he considered satisfactory reasons for his having been absent from his vessel. Megabates, however, was not satisfied, and refused to set Syclax at liberty. Aristagoras then told Megabates that he mistook his position in supposing that he was master of the expedition, and could tyrannize over the men in that manner, as he pleased. "I will have you understand," said he, "that I am the commander in this campaign, and that Artaphernes, in making you the sailing-master of the fleet, had no intention that you should set up your authority over mine." So saying, he went away in a rage, and released Syclax from his durance with his own hands.

It was now the turn of Megabates to be enraged. He determined to defeat the expedition. He sent immediately a secret messenger to warn the Naxians of their enemies' approach. The Naxians immediately made effectual preparations to defend themselves. The end of it was, that when the fleet arrived, the island was prepared to receive it, and nothing could be done. Aristagoras continued the siege four months; but inasmuch as, during all this time, Megabates did every thing in his power to circumvent and thwart every plan that Aristagoras formed, nothing was accomplished. Finally, the expedition was broken up, and Aristagoras returned home, disappointed and chagrined, all his hopes blasted, and his own private finances thrown into confusion by the great pecuniary losses which he himself had sustained. He had contributed very largely, from his own private funds, in fitting out the expedition, fully confident of success, and of ample reimbursement for his expenses as the consequence of it.

He was angry with himself, and angry with Megabates, and angry with Artaphernes. He presumed, too, that Megabates would denounce him to Artaphernes, and, through him, to Darius, as the cause of the failure of the expedition. A sudden order might come at any moment, directing that he should be beheaded. He began to consider the expediency of revolting from the Persian power, and making common cause with the Greeks against Darius. The danger of such a step was scarcely less than that of remaining as he was. While he was pondering these momentous questions in his mind, he was led suddenly to a decision by a very singular circumstance, the proper explaining of which requires the story to return, for a time, to Histis at Susa.

Histis was very ill at ease in the possession of his forced elevation and grandeur at Susa. He enjoyed great distinction there, it is true, and a life of ease and luxury, but he wished for independence and authority. He was, accordingly, very desirous to get back to his former sphere of activity and power in Asia Minor. After revolving in his mind the various plans which occurred to him for accomplishing this purpose, he at last decided on inducing Aristagoras to revolt in Ionia, and then attempting to persuade Darius to send him on to quell the revolt. When once in Asia Minor, he would join the rebellion, and bid Darius defiance.

The first thing to be done was to contrive some safe and secret way to communicate with Aristagoras. This he effected in the following manner: There was a man in his court who was afflicted with some malady of the eyes. Histis told him that if he would put himself under his charge he could effect a cure. It would be necessary, he said, that the man should have his head shaved and scarified; that is, punctured with a sharp instrument, previously dipped in some medicinal compound. Then, after some further applications should have been made, it would be necessary for the patient to go to Ionia, in Asia Minor, where there was a physician who would complete the cure.

The patient consented to this proposal. The head was shaved, and Histis, while pretending to scarify it, pricked into the skin--as sailors tattoo anchors on their arms--by means of a needle and a species of ink which had probably no great medicinal virtue, the words of a letter to Aristagoras, in which he communicated to him fully, though very concisely, the particulars of his plan. He urged Aristagoras to revolt, and promised that, if he would do so, he would come on, himself, as soon as possible, and, under pretense of marching to suppress the rebellion, he would really join and aid it.

As soon as he had finished pricking this treasonable communication into the patient's skin, he carefully enveloped the head in bandages, which, he said, must on no account be disturbed. He kept the man shut up, besides, in the palace, until the hair had grown, so as effectually to conceal the writing, and then sent him to Ionia to have the cure perfected. On his arrival at Ionia he was to find Aristagoras, who would do what further was necessary. Histis contrived, in the mean time, to send word to Aristagoras by another messenger, that, as soon as such a patient should present himself, Aristagoras was to shave his head. He did so, and the communication appeared. We must suppose that the operations on the part of Aristagoras for the purpose of completing the cure consisted, probably, in pricking in more ink, so as to confuse and obliterate the writing.

Aristagoras was on the eve of throwing off the Persian authority when he received this communication. It at once decided him to proceed. He organized his forces and commenced his revolt. As soon as the news of this rebellion reached Susa, Histis feigned great indignation, and earnestly entreated Darius to commission him to go and suppress it. He was confident, he said, that he could do it in a very prompt and effectual manner. Darius was at first inclined to suspect that Histis was in some way or other implicated in the movement; but these suspicions were removed by the protestations which Histis made, and at length he gave him leave to proceed to Miletus, commanding him, however, to return to Susa again as soon as he should have suppressed the revolt.

When Histis arrived in Ionia he joined Aristagoras, and the two generals, leaguing with them various princes and states of Greece, organized a very extended and dangerous rebellion, which it gave the troops of Darius infinite trouble to subdue. We can not here give an account of the incidents and particulars of this war. For a time the rebels prospered, and their cause seemed likely to succeed; but at length the tide turned against them. Their towns were captured, their ships were taken and destroyed, their armies cut to pieces. Histis retreated from place to place, a wretched fugitive, growing more and more distressed and destitute every day. At length, as he was flying from a battle field, he arrested the arm of a Persian, who was pursuing him with his weapon upraised, by crying out that he was Histis the Milesian. The Persian, hearing this, spared his life, but took him prisoner, and delivered him to Artaphernes. Histis begged very earnestly that Artaphernes would send him to Darius alive, in hopes that Darius would pardon him in consideration of his former services at the bridge of the Danube. This was, however, exactly what Artaphernes wished to prevent; so he crucified the wretched Histis at Sardis, and then packed his head in salt and sent it to Darius.

CHAPTER XI.

THE INVASION OF GREECE AND THE BATTLE OF MARATHON.

B.C. 512-490

Great battles.--Progress of the Persian empire.--Condition of the Persian empire.--Plans of Darius.--Persian power in Thrace.--Attempted negotiation with Macedon.--The seven commissioners.--Their rudeness at the feast.--Stratagem of Amyntas's son.--The commissioners killed.--Artifice of the prince.--Darius's anger against the Athenians.--Civil dissensions in Greece.--The tyrants.--Periander.--His message to a neighboring potentate.--Periander's intolerable tyranny.--His wife Melissa.--The ghost of Melissa.--A great sacrifice.--The reason of Periander's rudeness to the assembly of females.--Labda the cripple.--Prediction in respect to her progeny.--Conspiracy to destroy Labda's child.--Its failure.--The child secreted.--Fulfillment of the oracle.--Hippias of Athens.--His barbarous cruelty.--Hippias among the Persians.--Wars between the Grecian states.--Quarrel between Athens and Aina.--The two wooden statues.--Incursion of the Ainetans.--They carry off the statues.--Attempt to recover the statues.--They fall upon their knees.--The Athenian fugitive.--He is murdered by the women.--The Persian army.--Its commander, Datis.--Sailing of the fleet.--Various conquests.--Landing of the Persians.--State of Athens.--The Greek army.--Miltiades and his colleagues.--Position of the armies.--Miltiades's plan of attack.--Onset of the Greeks.--Rout of the Persians.--Results of the battle.--Numbers slain.--The field of Marathon.--The mound.--Song of the Greek.

In the history of a great military conqueror, there seems to be often some one great battle which in importance and renown eclipses all the rest. In the case of Hannibal it was the battle of Cann? in that of Alexander the battle of Arbela. Caesar's great conflict was at Pharsalia, Napoleon's at Waterloo. Marathon was, in some respects, Darius's Waterloo. The place is a beautiful plain, about twelve miles north of the great city of Athens. The battle was the great final contest between Darius and the Greeks, which, both on account of the awful magnitude of the conflict, and the very extraordinary circumstances which attended it, has always been greatly celebrated among mankind.

The whole progress of the Persian empire, from the time of the first accession of Cyrus to the throne, was toward the westward, till it reached the confines of Asia on the shores of the 炎 ean Sea. All the shores and islands of this sea were occupied by the states and the cities of Greece. The population of the whole region, both on the European and Asiatic shores, spoke the same language, and possessed the same vigorous, intellectual, and elevated character. Those on the Asiatic side had been conquered by Cyrus, and their countries had been annexed to the Persian empire. Darius had wished very strongly, at the commencement of his reign, to go on in this work of annexation, and had sent his party of commissioners to explore the ground, as is related in a preceding chapter. He had, however, postponed the execution of his plans, in order first to conquer the Scythian countries north of Greece, thinking, probably, that this would make the subsequent conquest of Greece itself more easy. By getting a firm foothold in Scythia, he would, as it were, turn the flank of the Grecian territories, which would tend to make his final descent upon them more effectual and sure.

This plan, however, failed; and yet, on his retreat from Scythia, Darius did not withdraw his armies wholly from the European side of the water. He kept a large force in Thrace, and his generals there were gradually extending and strengthening their power, and preparing for still greater conquests. They attempted to extend their dominion, sometimes by negotiations, and sometimes by force, and they were successful and unsuccessful by turns, whichever mode they employed.

One very extraordinary story is told of an attempted negotiation with Macedon, made with a view of bringing that kingdom, if possible, under the Persian dominion, without the necessity of a resort to force. The commanding general of Darius's armies in Thrace, whose name, as was stated in the last chapter, was Megabyzus, sent seven Persian officers into Macedon, not exactly to summon the Macedonians, in a peremptory manner, to surrender to the Persians, nor, on the other hand, to propose a voluntary alliance, but for something between the two. The communication was to be in the form of a proposal, and yet it was to be made in the domineering and overbearing manner with which the tyrannical and the strong often make proposals to the weak and defenseless.

The seven Persians went to Macedon, which, as will be seen from the map, was west of Thrace, and to the northward of the other Grecian countries. Amyntas, the king of Macedon, gave them a very honorable reception. At length, one day, at a feast to which they were invited in the palace of Amyntas, they became somewhat excited with wine, and asked to have the ladies of the court brought into the apartment. They wished "to see them," they said. Amyntas replied that such a procedure was entirely contrary to the usages and customs of their court; but still, as he stood somewhat in awe of his visitors, or, rather, of the terrible power which the delegation represented, and wished by every possible means to avoid provoking a quarrel with them, he consented to comply with their request. The ladies were sent for. They came in, reluctant and blushing, their minds excited by mingled feelings of indignation and shame.

The Persians, becoming more and more excited and imperious under the increasing influence of the wine, soon began to praise the beauty of these new guests in a coarse and free manner, which overwhelmed the ladies with confusion, and then to accost them familiarly and rudely, and to behave toward them, in other respects, with so much impropriety as to produce great alarm and indignation among all the king's household. The king himself was much distressed, but he was afraid to act decidedly. His son, a young man of great energy and spirit, approached his father with a countenance and manner expressive of high excitement, and begged him to retire from the feast, and leave him, the son, to manage the affair. Amyntas reluctantly allowed himself to be persuaded to go, giving his son many charges, as he went away, to do nothing rashly or violently. As soon as the king was gone, the prince made an excuse for having the ladies retire for a short time, saying that they should soon return. The prince conducted them to their apartment, and then selecting an equal number of tall and smooth-faced boys, he disguised them to represent the ladies, and gave each one a dagger, directing him to conceal it beneath his robe. These counterfeit females were then introduced to the assembly in the place of those who had retired. The Persians did not detect the deception. It was evening, and, besides, their faculties were confused with the effects of the wine. They approached the supposed ladies as they had done before, with rude familiarity; and the boys, at a signal made by the prince when the Persians were wholly off their guard, stabbed and killed every one of them on the spot.

Megabyzus sent an embassador to inquire what became of his seven messengers; but the Macedonian prince contrived to buy this messenger off by large rewards, and to induce him to send back some false but plausible story to satisfy Megabyzus. Perhaps Megabyzus would not have been so easily satisfied had it not been that the great Ionian rebellion, under Aristagoras and Histis, as described in the last chapter, broke out soon after, and demanded his attention in another quarter of the realm.

The Ionian rebellion postponed, for a time, Darius's designs on Greece, but the effect of it was to make the invasion more certain and more terrible in the end; for Athens, which was at that time one of the most important and powerful of the Grecian cities, took a part in that rebellion against the Persians. The Athenians sent forces to aid those of Aristagoras and Histis, and, in the course of the war, the combined army took and burned the city of Sardis. When this news reached Darius, he was excited to a perfect phrensy of resentment and indignation against the Athenians for coming thus into his own dominions to assist rebels, and there destroying one of his most important capitals. He uttered the most violent and terrible threats against them, and, to prevent his anger from getting cool before the preparations should be completed for vindicating it, he made an arrangement, it was said, for having a slave call out to him every day at table, "Remember the Athenians!"

It was a circumstance favorable to Darius's designs against the states of Greece that they were not united among themselves. There was no general government under which the whole naval and military force of that country could be efficiently combined, so as to be directed, in a concentrated and energetic form, against a common enemy. On the other hand, the several cities formed, with the territories adjoining them, so many separate states, more or less connected, it is true, by confederations and alliances, but still virtually independent, and often hostile to each other. Then, besides these external and international quarrels, there was a great deal of internal dissension. The monarchical and the democratic principle were all the time struggling for the mastery. Military despots were continually rising to power in the various cities, and after they had ruled, for a time, over their subjects with a rod of iron, the people would rise in rebellion and expel them from their thrones. These revolutions were continually taking place, attended, often, by the strangest and most romantic incidents, which evinced, on the part of the actors in them, that extraordinary combination of mental sagacity and acumen with childish and senseless superstition so characteristic of the times.

It is not surprising that the populace often rebelled against the power of these royal despots, for they seem to have exercised their power, when their interests or their passions excited them to do it, in the most tyrannical and cruel manner. One of them, it was said, a king of Corinth, whose name was Periander, sent a messenger, on one occasion, to a neighboring potentate--

with whom he had gradually come to entertain very friendly relations--to inquire by what means he could most certainly and permanently secure the continuance of his power. The king thus applied to gave no direct reply, but took the messenger out into his garden, talking with him by the way about the incidents of his journey, and other indifferent topics. He came, at length, to a field where grain was growing, and as he walked along, he occupied himself in cutting off, with his sword, every head of the grain which raised itself above the level of the rest. After a short time he returned to the house, and finally dismissed the messenger without giving him any answer whatever to the application that he had made. The messenger returned to Periander, and related what had occurred. "I understand his meaning," said Periander. "I must contrive some way to remove all those who, by their talents, their influence, or their power, rise above the general level of the citizens." Periander began immediately to act on this recommendation. Whoever, among the people of Corinth, distinguished himself above the rest, was marked for destruction. Some were banished, some were slain, and some were deprived of their influence, and so reduced to the ordinary level, by the confiscation of their property, the lives and fortunes of all the citizens of the state being wholly in the despot's hands.

This same Periander had a wife whose name was Melissa. A very extraordinary tale is related respecting her, which, though mainly fictitious, had a foundation, doubtless, in fact, and illustrates very remarkably the despotic tyranny and the dark superstition of the times. Melissa died and was buried; but her garments, for some reason or other, were not burned, as was usual in such cases. Now, among the other oracles of Greece, there was one where departed spirits could be consulted. It was called the oracle of the dead. Periander, having occasion to consult an oracle in order to find the means of recovering a certain article of value which was lost, sent to this place to call up and consult the ghost of Melissa. The ghost appeared, but refused to answer the question put to her, saying, with frightful solemnity,

"I am cold; I am cold; I am naked and cold. My clothes were not burned; I am naked and cold."

When this answer was reported to Periander, he determined to make a great sacrifice and offering, such as should at once appease the restless spirit. He invited, therefore, a general assembly of the women of Corinth to witness some spectacle in a temple, and when they were convened, he surrounded them with his guards, seized them, stripped them of most of their clothing, and then let them go free. The clothes thus taken were then all solemnly burned, as an expiatory offering, with invocations to the shade of Melissa.

The account adds, that when this was done, a second messenger was dispatched to the oracle of the dead, and the spirit, now clothed and comfortable in its grave, answered the inquiry, informing Periander where the lost article might be found.

The rude violence which Periander resorted to in this case seems not to have been dictated by any particular desire to insult or injure the women of Corinth, but was resorted to simply as the easiest and most convenient way of obtaining what he needed. He wanted a supply of valuable and costly female apparel, and the readiest mode of obtaining it was to bring together an assembly of females dressed for a public occasion, and then disrobe them. The case only shows to what an extreme and absolute supremacy the lofty and domineering spirit of ancient despotism attained.

It ought, however, to be related, in justice to these abominable tyrants, that they often evinced feelings of commiseration and kindness; sometimes, in fact, in very singular ways. There was, for example, in one of the cities, a certain family that had obtained the ascendency over the rest of the people, and had held it for some time as an established aristocracy, taking care to preserve their rank and power from generation to generation, by intermarrying only with one another. At length, in one branch of the family, there grew up a young girl named Labda, who had been a cripple from her birth, and, on account of her deformity, none of the nobles would marry her. A man of obscure birth, however, one of the common people, at length took her for his wife. His name was Eetion. One day, Eetion went to Delphi to consult an oracle, and as he was entering the temple, the Pythian[J] called out to him, saying that a stone should proceed from Labda which should overwhelm tyrants and usurpers, and free the state. The nobles, when they heard of this, understood the prediction to mean that the destruction of their power was, in some way or other, to be effected by means of Labda's child, and they determined to prevent the fulfillment of the prophecy by destroying the babe itself so soon as it should be born.

They accordingly appointed ten of their number to go to the place where Eetion lived and kill the child. The method which they were to adopt was this: They were to ask to see the infant on their arrival at the house, and then it was agreed that whichever of the ten it was to whom the babe was handed, he should dash it down upon the stone floor with all his force, by which means it would, as they supposed, certainly be killed.

This plan being arranged, the men went to the house, inquired, with hypocritical civility, after the health of the mother, and desired to see the child. It was accordingly brought to them. The mother put it into the hands of one of the conspirators, and the babe looked up into his face and smiled. This mute expression of defenseless and confiding innocence touched the murderer's heart. He could not be such a monster as to dash such an image of trusting and happy helplessness upon the stones. He looked upon the child, and then gave it into the hands of the one next to him, and he gave it to the next, and thus it passed through the hands of all the ten. No one was found stern and determined enough to murder it, and at last they gave the babe back to its mother and went away.

The sequel of this story was, that the conspirators, when they reached the gate, stopped to consult together, and after many mutual criminations and recriminations, each impugning the courage and resolution of the rest, and all joining in special condemnation of the man to whom the child had at first been given, they went back again, determined, in some way or other, to accomplish their purpose. But Labda had, in the mean time, been alarmed at their extraordinary behavior, and had listened, when they stopped at the gate, to hear their conversation. She hastily hid the babe in a corn measure; and the conspirators, after looking in every part of the house in vain, gave up the search, supposing that their intended victim had been hastily sent away. They went home, and not being willing to acknowledge that their resolution had failed at the time of trial, they agreed to say that their undertaking had succeeded, and that the child had been destroyed. The babe lived, however, and grew up to manhood, and then, in fulfillment of the prediction announced by the oracle, he headed a rebellion against the nobles, deposed them from their power, and reigned in their stead.

One of the worst and most reckless of the Greek tyrants of whom we have been speaking was Hippias of Athens. His father, Pisistratus, had been hated all his life for his cruelties and his crimes; and when he died, leaving two sons, Hippias and Hipparchus, a conspiracy was formed to kill the sons, and thus put an end to the dynasty. Hipparchus was killed, but Hippias escaped the danger, and seized the government himself alone. He began to exercise his power in the most cruel and wanton manner, partly under the influence of resentment and passion, and partly because he thought his proper policy was to strike terror into the hearts of the people as a means of retaining his dominion. One of the conspirators by whom his brother had been slain, accused Hippias's warmest and best friends as his accomplices in that deed, in order to revenge himself on Hippias by inducing him to destroy his own adherents and supporters. Hippias fell into the snare; he condemned to death all whom the conspirator accused, and his reckless soldiers executed his friends and foes together. When any protested their innocence, he put them to the torture to make them confess their guilt. Such indiscriminate cruelty only had the effect to league the whole population of Athens against the perpetrator of it. There was at length a general insurrection against him, and he was dethroned. He made his escape to Sardis, and there tendered his services to Artaphernes, offering to conduct the Persian armies to Greece, and aid them in getting possession of the country, on condition that, if they succeeded, the Persians would make him the governor of Athens. Artaphernes made known these offers to Darius, and they were eagerly accepted. It was, however, very impolitic to accept them. The aid which the invaders could derive from the services of such a guide, were far more than counterbalanced by the influence which his defection and the espousal of his cause by the Persians would produce in Greece. It banded the Athenians and their allies together in the most enthusiastic and determined spirit of resistance, against a man who had now added the baseness of treason to the wanton wickedness of tyranny.

Besides these internal dissensions between the people of the several Grecian states and their kings, there were contests between one state and another, which Darius proposed to take advantage of in his attempts to conquer the country. There was one such war in particular, between Athens and the island of Aina, on the effects of which, in aiding him in his operations against the Athenians, Darius placed great reliance. Aina was a large and populous island not far from Athens. In accounting for the origin of the quarrel between the two states, the Greek historians relate the following marvelous story:

Aina, as will be seen from the map, was situated in the middle of a bay, southwest from Athens. On the other side of the bay, opposite from Athens, there was a city, near the shore, called Epidaurus. It happened that the people of Epidaurus were at one time suffering from famine, and they sent a messenger to the oracle at Delphi to inquire what they should do to obtain relief. The Pythian answered that they must erect two statues to certain goddesses, named Damia and Auxesia, and that then the famine would abate. They asked whether they were to make the statues of brass or of marble. The priestess replied, "Of neither, but of wood." They were, she said, to use for the purpose the wood of the garden olive.

This species of olive was a sacred tree, and it happened that, at this time, there were no trees of the kind that were of sufficient size for the purpose intended except at Athens; and the Epidaurians, accordingly, sent to Athens to obtain leave to supply themselves with wood for the sculptor by cutting down one of the trees from the sacred grove. The Athenians consented to this, on condition that the Epidaurians would offer a certain yearly sacrifice at two temples in Athens, which they named. This sacrifice, they seemed to imagine, would make good to the city whatever of injury their religious interests might suffer from the loss of the sacred tree. The Epidaurians agreed to the condition; the tree was felled; blocks from it, of proper size, were taken to Epidaurus, and the statues were carved. They were set up in the city with the usual solemnities, and the famine soon after disappeared.

Not many years after this, a war, for some cause or other, broke out between Epidaurus and 炗 ina. The people of 炗 ina crossed the water in a fleet of galleys, landed at Epidaurus, and, after committing various ravages, they seized these images, and bore them away in triumph as trophies of their victory. They set them up in a public place in the middle of their own island, and instituted games and spectacles around them, which they celebrated with great festivity and parade. The Epidaurians, having thus lost their statues, ceased to make the annual offering at Athens which they had stipulated for, in return for receiving the wood from which the statues were carved. The Athenians complained. The Epidaurians replied that they had continued to make the offering as long as they had kept the statues; but that now, the statues being in other hands, they were absolved from the obligation. The Athenians next demanded the statues themselves of the people of 荑 ina. They refused to surrender them. The Athenians then invaded the island, and proceeded to the spot where the statues had been erected. They had been set up on massive and heavy pedestals. The Athenians attempted to get them down, but could not separate them from their fastenings. They then changed their plan, and undertook to move the pedestals too, by dragging them with ropes. They were arrested in this undertaking by an earthquake, accompanied by a solemn and terrible sound of thunder, which warned them that they were provoking the anger of Heaven.

The statues, too, miraculously fell on their knees, and remained fixed in that posture!

The Athenians, terrified at these portentous signs, abandoned their undertaking and fled toward the shore. They were, however, intercepted by the people of 荑 ina, and some allies whom they had hastily summoned to their aid, and the whole party was destroyed except one single man. He escaped.

This single fugitive, however, met with a worse fate than that of his comrades. He went to Athens, and there the wives and sisters of the men who had been killed thronged around him to hear his story. They were incensed that he alone had escaped, as if his flight had been a sort of betrayal and desertion of his companions. They fell upon him, therefore, with one accord, and pierced and wounded him on all sides with a sort of pin, or clasp, which they used as a fastening for their dress. They finally killed him.

The Athenian magistrates were unable to bring any of the perpetrators of this crime to conviction and punishment; but a law was made, in consequence of the occurrence, forbidding the use of that sort of fastening for the dress to all the Athenian women forever after. The people of 荑 ina, on the other hand, rejoiced and gloried in the deed of the Athenian women, and they made the clasps which were worn upon their island of double size, in honor of it.

The war, thus commenced between Athens and 荑 ina, went on for a long time, increasing in bitterness and cruelty as the injuries increased in number and magnitude which the belligerent parties inflicted on each other.

Such was the state of things in Greece when Darius organized his great expedition for the invasion of the country. He assembled an immense armament, though he did not go forth himself to command it. He placed the whole force under the charge of a Persian general named Datis. A considerable part of the army which Datis was to command was raised in Persia; but orders had been sent on that large accessions to the army, consisting of cavalry, foot soldiers, ships, and seamen, and every other species of military force, should be raised in all the provinces of Asia Minor, and be ready to join it at various places of rendezvous.

Darius commenced his march at Susa with the troops which had been collected there, and proceeded westward till he reached the Mediterranean at Cilicia, which is at the northeast corner of that sea. Here large re-enforcements joined him; and there was also assembled at this point an immense fleet of galleys, which had been provided to convey the troops to the Grecian seas. The troops embarked, and the fleet advanced along the southern shores of Asia Minor to the 灾 ean Sea, where they turned to the northward toward the island of Samos, which had been appointed as a rendezvous. At Samos they were joined by still greater numbers coming from Ionia, and the various provinces and islands on that coast that were already under the Persian dominion. When they were ready for their final departure, the immense fleet, probably one of the greatest and most powerful which had then ever been assembled, set sail, and steered their course to the northwest, among the islands of the 灾 ean Sea. As they moved slowly on, they stopped to take possession of such islands as came in their way. The islanders, in some cases, submitted to them without a struggle. In others, they made vigorous but perfectly futile attempts to resist. In others still, the terrified inhabitants abandoned their homes, and fled in dismay to the fastnesses of the mountains. The Persians destroyed the cities and towns whose inhabitants they could not conquer, and took the children from the most influential families of the islands which they did subdue, as hostages to hold their parents to their promises when their conquerors should have gone.

The mighty fleet advanced thus, by slow degrees, from conquest to conquest, toward the Athenian shores. The vast multitude of galleys covered the whole surface of the water, and as they advanced, propelled each by a triple row of oars, they exhibited to the fugitives who had gained the summits of the mountains the appearance of an immense swarm of insects, creeping, by an almost imperceptible advance, over the smooth expanse of the sea.

The fleet, guided all the time by Hippias, passed on, and finally entered the strait between the island of Euboea and the main land to the northward of Athens. Here, after some operations on the island, the Persians finally brought their ships into a port on the Athenian side, and landed. Hippias made all the arrangements, and superintended the disembarkation.

In the mean time, all was confusion and dismay in the city of Athens. The government, as soon as they heard of the approach of this terrible danger, had sent an express to the city of Sparta, asking for aid. The aid had been promised, but it had not yet arrived. The Athenians gathered together all the forces at their command on the northern side of the city, and were debating the question, with great anxiety and earnestness, whether they should shut themselves up within the walls, and await the onset of their enemies there, or go forth to meet them on the way. The whole force which the Greeks could muster consisted of but about ten thousand men, while the Persian host contained over a hundred thousand. It seemed madness to engage in a contest on an open field against such an overwhelming disparity of numbers. A majority of voices were, accordingly, in favor of remaining within the fortifications of the city, and awaiting an attack.

The command of the army had been intrusted, not to one man, but to a commission of three generals, a sort of triumvirate, on whose joint action the decision of such a question devolved. Two of the three were in favor of taking a defensive position; but the third, the celebrated Miltiades, was so earnest and so decided in favor of attacking the enemy themselves, instead of waiting to be attacked, that his opinion finally carried the day, and the other generals resigned their portion of authority into his hands, consenting that he should lead the Greek army into battle, if he dared to take the responsibility of doing so.

The two armies were at this time encamped in sight of each other on the plain of Marathon, between the mountain and the sea. They were nearly a mile apart. The countless multitude of the Persians extended as far as the eye could reach, with long lines of tents in the distance, and thousands of horsemen on the plain, all ready for the charge. The Greeks, on the other hand, occupied a small and isolated spot, in a compact form, without cavalry, without archers, without, in fact, any weapons suitable either for attack or defense, except in a close encounter hand to hand. Their only hope of success depended on the desperate violence of the onset they were to make upon the vast masses of men spread out before them. On the one side were immense numbers, whose force, vast as it was, must necessarily be more or less impeded in its operations, and slow. It was to be overpowered, therefore, if overpowered at all, by the utmost fierceness and rapidity of action--by sudden onsets, unexpected and furious assaults, and heavy, vigorous, and rapid blows. Miltiades, therefore, made all his arrangements with reference to that mode of warfare. Such soldiers as the Greeks, too, were admirably adapted to execute such designs, and the immense and heterogeneous mass of Asiatic nations which covered the plain before them was exactly the body for such an experiment to be made upon. Glorying in their numbers and confident of victory, they were slowly advancing, without the least idea that the little band before them could possibly do them any serious harm. They had actually brought with them, in the train of the army, some blocks of marble, with which they were going to erect a monument of their victory, on the field of battle, as soon as the conflict was over!

At length the Greeks began to put themselves in motion. As they advanced, they accelerated their march more and more, until just before reaching the Persian lines, when they began to run. The astonishment of the Persians at this unexpected and daring onset soon gave place, first to the excitement of personal conflict, and then to universal terror and dismay; for the headlong impetuosity of the Greeks bore down all opposition, and the desperate swordsmen cut their way through the vast masses of the enemy with a fierce and desperate fury that nothing could withstand. Something like a contest continued for some hours; but, at the end of that time, the Persians were flying in all directions, every one endeavoring, by the track which he found most practicable for himself, to make his way to the ships on the shore. Vast multitudes were killed in this headlong flight; others became entangled in the morasses and fens, and others still strayed away, and sought, in their terror, a hopeless refuge in the defiles of the mountains. Those who escaped crowded in confusion on board their ships, and pushed off from the shore, leaving the whole plain covered with their dead and dying companions.

The Greeks captured an immense amount of stores and baggage, which were of great cost and value. They took possession, too, of the marble blocks which the Persians had brought to immortalize their victory, and built with them a monument, instead, to commemorate their defeat. They counted the dead. Six thousand Persians, and only two hundred Greeks, were found. The bodies of the Greeks were collected together, and buried on the field, and an immense mound was raised over the grave. This mound has continued to stand at Marathon to the present day.

The battle of Marathon was one of those great events in the history of the human race which continue to attract, from age to age, the admiration of mankind. They who look upon war, in all its forms, as only the perpetration of an unnatural and atrocious crime, which rises to dignity and grandeur only by the very enormity of its guilt, can not but respect the courage, the energy, and the cool and determined resolution with which the little band of Greeks went forth to stop the torrent of foes which all the nations of a whole continent had combined to pour upon them. The field has been visited in every age by thousands of travelers, who have upon the spot offered their tribute of admiration to the ancient heroes that triumphed there. The plain is found now, as of old, overlooking the sea, and the mountains inland, towering above the plain. The mound, too, still remains, which was reared to consecrate the memory of the Greeks who fell. They who visit it stand and survey the now silent and solitary scene, and derive from the influence and spirit of the spot new strength and energy to meet the great difficulties and dangers of life which they themselves have to encounter. The Greeks themselves, of the present day, notwithstanding the many sources of discouragement and depression with which they have to contend, must feel at Marathon some rising spirit of emulation in contemplating the lofty mental powers and the undaunted spirit of their sires. Byron makes one of them sing,

"The mountains look on Marathon, And Marathon looks on the sea; And musing there an hour alone, I dreamed that Greece might still be free; For, standing on the Persians' grave, I could not deem myself a slave."

CHAPTER XII.

THE DEATH OF DARIUS.

The Persian fleet sails southward.--Fate of Hippias.--Omens.--The dream and the sneeze.--Hippias falls in battle.--Movements of the Persian fleet.--The Persian fleet returns to Asia.--Anxiety of Datis.--Datis finds a stolen statue.-- Island of Delos.--Account of the sacred island.--Its present condition.-- Disposition of the army.--Darius's reception of Datis.--Subsequent history of Miltiades.--His great popularity.--Miltiades's influence at Athens.--His ambitious designs.--Island and city of Paros.--Appearance of the modern town.--Miltiades's proposition to the Athenians.--They accept it.--Miltiades marches against Paros.--Its resistance.--Miltiades is discouraged.--The captive priestess.--Miltiades's interview with the priestess.--Her instructions.-- Miltiades attempts to enter the temple of Ceres.--He dislocates a limb.-- Miltiades returns to Athens.--He is impeached.--Miltiades is condemned.--He dies of his wound.--The fine paid.--Proposed punishment of Timo.--Timo saved by the Delphic oracle.--Another expedition against Greece.-- Preparations.--Necessity for settling the succession.--Darius's two sons.--Their claims to the throne.--Xerxes declared heir.--Death of Darius.--Character of Darius.--Ground of his renown.

The city of Athens and the plain of Marathon are situated upon a peninsula. The principal port by which the city was ordinarily approached was on the southern shore of the peninsula, though the Persians had landed on the northern side. Of course, in their retreat from the field of battle, they fled to the north. When they were beyond the reach of their enemies and fairly at sea, they were at first somewhat perplexed to determine what to do. Datis was extremely unwilling to return to Darius with the news of such a defeat. On the other hand, there seemed but little hope of any other result if he were to attempt a second landing.

Hippias, their Greek guide, was killed in the battle. He expected to be killed, for his mind, on the morning of the battle, was in a state of great despondency and dejection. Until that time he had felt a strong and confident expectation of success, but his feelings had then been very suddenly changed. His confidence had arisen from the influence of a dream, his dejection from a cause more frivolous still; so that he was equally irrational in his hope and in his despair.

The omen which seemed to him to portend success to the enterprise in which he had undertaken to act as guide, was merely that he dreamed one night that he saw, and spent some time in company with, his mother. In attempting to interpret this dream in the morning, it seemed to him that Athens, his native city, was represented by his mother, and that the vision denoted that he was about to be restored to Athens again. He was extremely elated at this supernatural confirmation of his hopes, and would have gone into the battle certain of victory, had it not been that another circumstance occurred at the time of the landing to blast his hopes. He had, himself, the general charge of the disembarkation. He stationed the ships at their proper places near the shore, and formed the men upon the beach as they landed. While he was thus engaged, standing on the sand, he suddenly sneezed. He was an old man, and his teeth--those that remained--were loose. One of them was thrown out in the act of sneezing, and it fell into the sand. Hippias was alarmed at this occurrence, considering it a bad omen. He looked a long time for the tooth in vain, and then exclaimed that all was over. The joining of his tooth to his mother earth was the event to which his dream referred, and there was now no hope of any further fulfillment of it. He went on mechanically, after this, in marshaling his men and preparing for battle, but his mind was oppressed with gloomy forebodings. He acted, in consequence, feebly and with indecision; and when the Greeks explored the field on the morning after the battle, his body was found among the other mutilated and ghastly remains which covered the ground.

As the Persian fleet moved, therefore, along the coast of Attica, they had no longer their former guide. They were still, however, very reluctant to leave the country. They followed the shore of the peninsula until they came to the promontory of Sunium, which forms the southeastern extremity of it. They doubled this cape, and then followed the southern shore of the peninsula until they arrived at the point opposite to Athens on that side. In the mean time, however, the Spartan troops which had been sent for to aid the Athenians in the contest, but which had not arrived in time to take part in the battle, reached the ground; and the indications which the Persians observed, from the decks of their galleys, that the country was thoroughly aroused, and was every where ready to receive them, deterred them from making any further attempts to land. After lingering, therefore, a short time near the shore, the fleet directed its course again toward the coasts of Asia.

The mind of Datis was necessarily very ill at ease. He dreaded the wrath of Darius; for despots are very prone to consider military failures as the worst of crimes. The expedition had not, however, been entirely a failure. Datis had conquered many of the Greek islands, and he had with him, on board his galleys, great numbers of prisoners, and a vast amount of plunder which he had obtained from them. Still, the greatest and most important of the objects which Darius had commissioned him to accomplish had been entirely defeated, and he felt, accordingly, no little anxiety in respect to the reception which he was to expect at Susa.

One night he had a dream which greatly disturbed him. He awoke in the morning with an impression upon his mind, which he had derived from the dream, that some temple had been robbed by his soldiers in the course of his expedition, and that the sacrilegious booty which had been obtained was concealed somewhere in the fleet. He immediately ordered a careful search to be instituted, in which every ship was examined. At length they found, concealed in one of the galleys, a golden statue of Apollo. Datis inquired what city it had been taken from. They answered from Delium. Delium was on the coast of Attica, near the place where the Persians had landed, at the time of their advance on Marathon. Datis could not safely or conveniently go back there to restore it to its place. He determined, therefore, to deposit it at Delos for safe keeping, until it could be returned to its proper home.

Delos was a small but very celebrated island near the center of the 犬 ean Sea, and but a short distance from the spot where the Persian fleet was lying when Datis made this discovery. It was a sacred island, devoted to religious rites, and all contention, and violence, and, so far as was possible, all suffering and death, were excluded from it. The sick were removed from it; the dead were not buried there; armed ships and armed men laid aside their hostility to each other when they approached it. Belligerent fleets rode at anchor, side by side, in peace, upon the smooth waters of its little port, and an enchanting picture of peace, tranquillity, and happiness was seen upon its shores. A large natural fountain, or spring, thirty feet in diameter, and inclosed partly by natural rocks and partly by an artificial wall, issued from the ground in the center of the island, and sent forth a beautiful and fertilizing rill into a rich and happy valley, through which it meandered, deviously, for several miles, seeking the sea. There was a large and populous city near the port, and the whole island was adorned with temples, palaces, colonnades, and other splendid architectural structures, which made it the admiration of all mankind. All this magnificence and beauty have, however, long since passed away. The island is now silent, deserted, and desolate, a dreary pasture, where cattle browse and feed, with stupid indifference, among the ancient ruins. Nothing living remains of the ancient scene of grandeur and beauty but the fountain. That still continues to pour up its clear and pellucid waters with a ceaseless and eternal flow.

It was to this Delos that Datis determined to restore the golden statue. He took it on board his own galley, and proceeded with it, himself, to the sacred island. He deposited it in the great temple of Apollo, charging the priests to convey it, as soon as a convenient opportunity should occur, to its proper destination at Delium.

The Persian fleet, after this business was disposed of, set sail again, and pursued its course toward the coasts of Asia, where at length the expedition landed in safety.

The various divisions of the army were then distributed in the different provinces where they respectively belonged, and Datis commenced his march with the Persian portion of the troops, and with his prisoners and plunder, for Susa, feeling, however, very uncertain how he should be received on his arrival there. Despotic power is always capricious; and the character of Darius, which seems to have been naturally generous and kind, and was rendered cruel and tyrannical only through the influence of the position in which he had been placed, was continually presenting the most opposite and contradictory phases. The generous elements of it, fortunately for Datis, seemed to be in the ascendency when the remnant of the Persian army arrived at Susa. Darius received the returning general without anger, and even treated the prisoners with humanity.

Before finally leaving the subject of this celebrated invasion, which was brought to an end in so remarkable a manner by the great battle of Marathon, it may be well to relate the extraordinary circumstances which attended the subsequent history of Miltiades, the great commander in that battle on the Greek side. Before the conflict, he seems to have had no official superiority over the other generals, but, by the resolute decision with which he urged the plan of giving the Persians battle, and the confidence and courage which he manifested in expressing his readiness to take the responsibility of the measure, he placed himself virtually at the head of the Greek command. The rest of the officers acquiesced in his pre-eminence, and, waiving their claims to an equal share of the authority, they allowed him to go forward and direct the operations of the day. If the day had been lost, Miltiades, even though he had escaped death upon the field, would have been totally and irretrievably ruined; but as it was won, the result of the transaction was that he was raised to the highest pinnacle of glory and renown.

And yet in this, as in all similar cases, the question of success or of failure depended upon causes wholly beyond the reach of human foresight or control. The military commander who acts in such contingencies is compelled to stake every thing dear to him on results which are often as purely hazardous as the casting of a die.

The influence of Miltiades in Athens after the Persian troops were withdrawn was paramount and supreme. Finding himself in possession of this ascendency, he began to form plans for other military undertakings. It proved, in the end, that it would have been far better for him to have been satisfied with the fame which he had already acquired.

Some of the islands in the 荥 ean Sea he considered as having taken part with the Persians in the invasion, to such an extent, at least, as to furnish him with a pretext for making war upon them. The one which he had specially in view, in the first instance, was Paros. Paros is a large and important island situated near the center of the southern portion of the 荥 ean Sea. It is of an oval form, and is about twelve miles long. The surface of the land is beautifully diversified and very picturesque, while, at the same time, the soil is very fertile. In the days of Miltiades, it was very wealthy and populous, and there was a large city, called also Paros, on the western coast of the island, near the sea. There is a modern town built upon the site of the former city, which presents a very extraordinary appearance, as the dwellings are formed, in a great measure, of materials obtained from the ancient ruins. Marble columns, sculptured capitals, and fragments of what were once magnificent entablatures, have been used to construct plain walls, or laid in obscure and neglected pavements--all, however, still retaining, notwithstanding their present degradation, unequivocal marks of the nobleness of their origin. The quarries where the ancient Parian marble was obtained were situated on this island, not very far from the town. They remain to the present day in the same state in which the ancient workmen left them.

In the time of Miltiades the island and the city of Paros were both very wealthy and very powerful. Miltiades conceived the design of making a descent upon the island, and levying an immense contribution upon the people, in the form of a fine, for what he considered their treason in taking part with the enemies of their countrymen. In order to prevent the people of Paros from preparing for defense, Miltiades intended to keep the object of his expedition secret for a time. He therefore simply proposed to the Athenians that they should equip a fleet and put it under his command. He had an enterprise in view, he said, the nature of which he could not particularly explain, but he was very confident of its success, and, if successful, he should return, in a short time, laden with spoils which would enrich the city, and amply reimburse the people for the expenses they would have incurred. The force which he asked for was a fleet of seventy vessels.

So great was the popularity and influence which Miltiades had acquired by his victory at Marathon, that this somewhat extraordinary proposition was readily complied with. The fleet was equipped, and crews were provided, and the whole armament was placed under Miltiades's command. The men themselves who were embarked on board of the galleys did not know whither they were going. Miltiades promised them victory and an abundance of gold as their reward; for the rest, they must trust, he said, to him, as he could not explain the actual destination of the enterprise without endangering its success. The men were all satisfied with these conditions, and the fleet set sail.

When it arrived on the coast of Paros, the Parians were, of course, taken by surprise, but they made immediate preparations for a very vigorous resistance. Miltiades commenced a siege, and sent a herald to the city, demanding of them, as the price of their ransom, an immense sum of money, saying, at the same time, that, unless they delivered up that sum, or, at least, gave security for the payment of it, he would not leave the place until the city was captured, and, when captured, it should be wholly destroyed. The Parians rejected the demand, and engaged energetically in the work of completing and strengthening their defenses. They organized companies of workmen to labor during the night, when their operations would not be observed, in building new walls, and re-enforcing every weak or unguarded point in the line of the fortifications. It soon appeared that the Parians were making far more rapid progress in securing their position than Miltiades was in his assaults upon it. Miltiades found that an attack upon a fortified island in the 灾 ean Sea was a different thing from encountering the undisciplined hordes of Persians on the open plains of Marathon. There it was a contest between concentrated courage and discipline on the one hand, and a vast expansion of pomp and parade on the other; whereas now he found that the courage and discipline on his part were met by an equally indomitable resolution on the part of his opponents, guided, too, by an equally well-trained experience and skill. In a word, it was Greek against Greek at Paros, and Miltiades began at length to perceive that his prospect of success was growing very doubtful and dim.

This state of things, of course, filled the mind of Miltiades with great anxiety and distress; for, after the promises which he had made to the Athenians, and the blind confidence which he had asked of them in proposing that they should commit the fleet so unconditionally to his command, he could not return discomfited to Athens without involving himself in the most absolute disgrace. While he was in this perplexity, it happened that some of his soldiers took captive a Parian female, one day, among other prisoners. She proved to be a priestess, from one of the Parian temples. Her name was Timo. The thought occurred to Miltiades that, since all human means at his command had proved inadequate to accomplish his end, he might, perhaps, through this captive priestess, obtain some superhuman aid. As she had been in the service of a Parian temple, she would naturally have an influence with the divinities of the place, or, at least, she would be acquainted with the proper means of propitiating their favor.

Miltiades, accordingly, held a private interview with Timo, and asked her what he should do to propitiate the divinities of Paros so far as to enable him to gain possession of the city. She replied that she could easily point out the way, if he would but follow her instructions. Miltiades, overjoyed, promised readily that he would do so. She then gave him her instructions secretly. What they were is not known, except so far as they were revealed by the occurrences that followed.

There was a temple consecrated to the goddess Ceres near to the city, and so connected with it, it seems, as to be in some measure included within the defenses. The approach to this temple was guarded by a palisade. There were, however, gates which afforded access, except when they were fastened from within. Miltiades, in obedience to Timo's instructions, went privately, in the night, perhaps, and with very few attendants, to this temple. He attempted to enter by the gates, which he had expected, it seems, to find open. They were, however, fastened against him. He then undertook to scale the palisade. He succeeded in doing this, not, however, without difficulty, and then advanced toward the temple, in obedience to the instructions which he had received from Timo. The account states that the act, whatever it was, that Timo had directed him to perform, instead of being, as he supposed, a means of propitiating the favor of the divinity, was sacrilegious and impious; and Miltiades, as he approached the temple, was struck suddenly with a mysterious and dreadful horror of mind, which wholly overwhelmed him. Rendered almost insane by this supernatural remorse and terror, he turned to fly. He reached the palisade, and, in endeavoring to climb over it, his precipitation and haste caused him to fall. His attendants ran to take him up. He was helpless and in great pain. They found he had dislocated a joint in one of his limbs. He received, of course, every possible attention; but, instead of recovering from the injury, he found that the consequences of it became more and more serious every day. In a word, the great conqueror of the Persians was now wholly overthrown, and lay moaning on his couch as helpless as a child.

He soon determined to abandon the siege of Paros and return to Athens. He had been about a month upon the island, and had laid waste the rural districts, but, as the city had made good its defense against him, he returned without any of the rich spoil which he had promised. The disappointment which the people of Athens experienced on his arrival, turned soon into a feeling of hostility against the author of the calamity. Miltiades found that the fame and honor which he had gained at Marathon were gone. They had been lost almost as suddenly as they had been acquired. The rivals and enemies who had been silenced by his former success were now brought out and made clamorous against him by his present failure. They attributed the failure to his own mismanagement of the expedition, and one orator, at length, advanced articles of impeachment against him, on a charge of having been bribed by the Persians to make his siege of Paros only a feint. Miltiades could not defend himself from these criminations, for he was lying, at the time, in utter helplessness, upon his couch of pain. The dislocation of the limb had ended in an open wound, which at length, having resisted all the attempts of the physicians to stop its progress, had begun to mortify, and the life of the sufferer was fast ebbing away. His son Cimon did all in his power to save his father from both the dangers that threatened him. He defended his character in the public tribunals, and he watched over his person in the cell in the prison. These filial efforts were, however, in both cases unavailing. Miltiades was condemned by the tribunal, and he died of his wound.

The penalty exacted of him by the sentence was a very heavy fine. The sum demanded was the amount which the expedition to Paros had cost the city, and which, as it had been lost through the agency of Miltiades, it was adjudged that he should refund. This sentence, as well as the treatment in general which Miltiades received from his countrymen, has been since considered by mankind as very unjust and cruel. It was, however, only following out, somewhat rigidly, it is true, the essential terms and conditions of a military career. It results from principles inherent in the very nature of war, that we are never to look for the ascendency of justice and humanity in any thing pertaining to it. It is always power, and not right, that determines possession; it is success, not merit, that gains honors and rewards; and they who assent to the genius and spirit of military rule thus far, must not complain if they find that, on the same principle, it is failure and not crime which brings condemnation and destruction.

When Miltiades was dead, Cimon found that he could not receive his father's body for honorable interment unless he paid the fine. He had no means, himself, of doing this. He succeeded, however, at length, in raising the amount, by soliciting contributions from the family friends of his father. He paid the fine into the city treasury, and then the body of the hero was deposited in its long home.

The Parians were at first greatly incensed against the priestess Timo, as it seemed to them that she had intended to betray the city to Miltiades. They wished to put her to death, but they did not dare to do it. It might be considered an impious sacrilege to punish a priestess. They accordingly sent to the oracle at Delphi to state the circumstances of the case, and to inquire if they might lawfully put the priestess to death. She had been guilty, they said, of pointing out to an enemy the mode by which he might gain possession of their city; and, what was worse, she had, in doing so, attempted to admit him to those solemn scenes and mysteries in the temple which it was not lawful for any man to behold. The oracle replied that the priestess must not be punished, for she had done no wrong. It had been decreed by the gods that Miltiades should be destroyed, and Timo had been employed by them as the involuntary instrument of conducting him to his fate. The people of Paros acquiesced in this decision, and Timo was set free.

* * * * *

But to return to Darius. His desire to subdue the Greeks and to add their country to his dominions, and his determination to accomplish his purpose, were increased and strengthened, not diminished, by the repulse which his army had met with at the first invasion. He was greatly incensed against the Athenians, as if he considered their courage and energy in defending their country an audacious outrage against himself, and a crime. He resolved to organize a new expedition, still greater and more powerful than the other. Of this armament he determined to take the command himself in person, and to make the preparations for it on a scale of such magnitude as that the expedition should be worthy to be led by the great sovereign of half the world. He accordingly transmitted orders to all the peoples, nations, languages, and realms, in all his dominions, to raise their respective quotas of troops, horses, ships, and munitions of war, and prepare to assemble at such place of rendezvous as he should designate when all should be ready.

Some years elapsed before these arrangements were matured, and when at last the time seemed to have arrived for carrying his plans into effect, he deemed it necessary, before he commenced his march, to settle the succession of his kingdom; for he had several sons, who might each claim the throne, and involve the empire in disastrous civil wars in attempting to enforce their claims, in case he should never return. The historians say that there was a law of Persia forbidding the sovereign to leave the realm without previously fixing upon a successor. It is difficult to see, however, by what power or authority such a law could have been enacted, or to believe that monarchs like Darius would recognize an abstract obligation to law of any kind, in respect to their own political action. There is a species of law regulating the ordinary dealings between man and man, that springs up in all communities, whether savage or civilized, from custom, and from the action of judicial tribunals, which the most despotic and absolute sovereigns feel themselves bound, so far as relates to the private affairs of their subjects, to respect and uphold; but, in regard to their own personal and governmental acts and measures, they very seldom know any other authority than the impulses of their own sovereign will.

Darius had several sons, among whom there were two who claimed the right to succeed their father on the throne. One was the oldest son of a wife whom Darius had married before he became king. His name was Artobazanes. The other was the son of Atossa, the daughter of Cyrus, whom Darius had married after his accession to the throne. His name was Xerxes. Artobazanes claimed that he was entitled to be his father's heir, since he was his oldest son. Xerxes, on the other hand, maintained that, at the period of the birth of Artobazanes, Darius was not a king. He was then in a private station, and sons could properly inherit only what their fathers possessed at the time when they were born. He himself, on the other hand, was the oldest son which his father had had, being a king, and he was, consequently, the true inheritor of the kingdom. Besides, being the son of Atossa, he was the grandson of Cyrus, and the hereditary rights, therefore, of that great founder of the empire had descended to him.

Darius decided the question in favor of Xerxes, and then made arrangements for commencing his march, with a mind full of the elation and pride which were awakened by the grandeur of his position and the magnificence of his schemes. These schemes, however, he did not live to execute. He suddenly fell sick and died, just as he was ready to set out upon his expedition, and Xerxes, his son, reigned in his stead.

Xerxes immediately took command of the vast preparations which his father had made, and went on with the prosecution of the enterprise. The expedition which followed deserves, probably, in respect to the numbers engaged in it, the distance which it traversed, the immenseness of the expenses involved, and the magnitude of its results, to be considered the greatest military undertaking which human ambition and power have ever attempted to effect. The narrative, however, both of its splendid adventures and of its ultimate fate, belongs to the history of Xerxes.

The greatness of Darius was the greatness of position and not of character. He was the absolute sovereign of nearly half the world, and, as such, was held up very conspicuously to the attention of mankind, who gaze with a strong feeling of admiration and awe upon these vast elevations of power, as they do upon the summits of mountains, simply because they are high. Darius performed no great exploit, and he accomplished no great object while he lived; and he did not even leave behind him any strong impressions of personal character. There is in his history, and in the position which he occupies in the minds of men, greatness without dignity, success without merit, vast and long-continued power without effects accomplished or objects gained, and universal and perpetual renown without honor or applause. The world admire Caesar, Hannibal, Alexander, Alfred, and Napoleon for the deeds which they performed. They admire Darius only on account of the elevation on which he stood. In the same lofty position, they would have admired, probably, just as much, the very horse whose neighing placed him there.

THE END

Made in United States
Troutdale, OR
05/16/2024

19909711R00076